you have a place.

Murd Breg

RISE UP

Awaken the Leader in You

A Study of the Book of Nehemiah

MURIEL GREGORY

BROOKSTONE
PUBLISHING GROUP

RISE UP
Awaken the Leader in You
A Study of the Book of Nehemiah

Muriel Gregory

BROOKSTONE
PUBLISHING GROUP

Brookstone Publishing Group
P.O. Box 211, Evington, VA 24550
BrookstoneCreativeGxoup.com

ISBN: xxxxxxxxxxxx (paperback)

Ordering Information:
Special discounts are available on quantity purchases by corporations,
associations, and others. For details, contact
Brookstone Publishing Group at the address above.

CONTENTS

INTRODUCTION

DO YOU EVER FEEL LIKE IT'S BEST TO JUST KEEP YOUR HEAD down? Blend in? Keep a low profile? Or perhaps you're the exact opposite. You like to take charge. Inspire the masses. Lead from the front. Military life has a way of either bringing out the leader in us or relegating us to wallflower status. Maybe you're a little bit of both—a lion in uniform, but a mouse when it comes to building God's kingdom. Your service, dependent status, personality, family birth order, and life circumstances may dictate your identity and your behavior.

Nehemiah appears to have been a lion in both his vocation and his occupation. Temporarily leaving his post as cupbearer to the king, Nehemiah returns to his homeland only to find a burnt, dilapidated wall and discouraged, oppressed people. But rather than joining in the despair, Nehemiah elects to rise up to the calling God placed on his life. He inspires his people to rebuild the wall and restore their relationship with the God who had delivered them out of exile.

Much of the book of Nehemiah centers around Jerusalem in general and rebuilding its wall in particular. Several genealogical lists throughout the book contain list after list of names. God used musicians, priests, goldsmiths, perfumers, mighty men, daughters, and merchants. He also included dominating leaders like Nehemiah, shrinking violets like me, and everyone else who falls in between.

The God of the universe, who is all-powerful and all-knowing, uses fallible, fragile, and fickle people to carry out his mission here on earth. The four-star general, the Seaman Recruit, the military wife, the Staff Sergeant, the Marine veteran, the Academy grad, the Reservist, the Guardsman, and the proud military mom. God uses every one of us. And the mission didn't stop with Nehemiah's rebuilding of the wall in Jerusalem. God didn't say, "Good enough; let's stop here." No, he continued the story, showing us our desperate need for a Savior. Then, rather than leaving us in our mess, he sent the Savior, the God-man Jesus Christ. Through his atoning work on the cross, Jesus secured for us eternal life with God, which includes an abundance of other amazing benefits). He wants everyone to hear this good news. And he chooses you and me to spread his message.

God remains in the construction business—not simply building a wall, but establishing a people, a church, and a kingdom. If you're ready to pick up your hammer, God offers this opportunity for you to be part of his work. He's calling you to *Rise Up*.

What You Can Expect

In this six-week study, you will dig deeply into each chapter of the historical book of Nehemiah, finding God's faithfulness on every page. You will also examine themes such as prayer, integrity, leadership, justice, and worship. Content and application questions will help you mine the depths of this important book of the Bible. At the end of each chapter, you'll find a section called "Joint Op Intel." This will provide you with a bird's eye view of Nehemiah's contemporaries. Following that, you'll find "Habits to Outcome (H2O)," which will supply practical steps to help you apply what you've learned. As you study God's Word, we pray you will be encouraged and equipped to *Rise Up* to what God is calling you to do.

Please find a battle buddy to walk through this study with you. You are never alone at the wall.

Opposition, insurgency, and confusion will be on the horizon, but God promises to provide everything you need. All you have to do is *Rise Up*. Discover your place at the wall.

—MELISSA HICKS
MacDill AFB
Tampa, Florida

WEEK 1
Rise Up to The Call

Do you wish to rise? Begin by descending.
You plan a tower that will pierce the clouds? Lay first the foundation of humility.
—SAINT AUGUSTINE

On Hearing the Call

1427—Domrémy, France. A young girl struggled with vivid visions from God. First came the call to a pious life. Then came the call to reach out to the French king and lead his army against the English.

King Charles outfitted the 17-year-old Joan of Arc with armor and a horse, allowing her to accompany the army to Orléans, the site of an English siege. In a few months, the French defeated the English. Her military career advanced in a fast and forceful way, as she moved from victory to victory.

Without rank or education, Joan of Arc, a mere peasant girl, rose to God's call with courage and obedience. Her story demonstrates an important life lesson: Rising to the call is not linked to our social status or our current situation.

We can discover God's bigger purpose in our circumstances.

Does Anybody Else Witness This?

Few of us will ever get the call to lead a king's army against an enemy. At one point or another, however, we will sense a burden for a cause, a person, a country, or a situation. We may face a strong temptation to ignore the causes and needs around us. There might even be a palpable fear that we are not equipped for the job. We might be tempted to reject what we observe to protect ourselves or because we are scared. Closing our hearts and minds is not the answer. Rejecting the call is bypassing the blessing. As Aldous Huxley said, "facts do not cease to exist because they are ignored."

MISSION DEBRIEF

The book you are holding in your hands is a study on Nehemiah. He authored one of the historical books of the Old Testament. Even though he lived long ago in a distant land, we can learn a great deal from Nehemiah, because we have a lot in common with him. Have you ever received terrible news that crushed your spirit? Have you ever witnessed an injustice so profound that it moved you to tears? How about those people in your life whose sole purpose seems to be to make you stumble? Have you ever lacked the courage to do the right thing? You will come to love Nehemiah, as he confronts the challenges before him.

Nehemiah served in an advantageous position in the Persian Kingdom. Living a life of comfort and luxury, his world was turned upside down with a single announcement. About 140 years prior to this event, invading armies tore down the protective city wall, and fire destroyed the gates of Jerusalem. Hoping for news that his homeland was being restored, Nehemiah became distraught when his brother, Hanani, brought the devastating news that nothing had gotten better. He fell to his knees and wept.

The Call to Arms

"Now, I was a cupbearer to the king" (Nehemiah 1:11). Nehemiah penned those words at the end of the first chapter we will read this week. This statement reveals much more than a job description. A man in such proximity to the king had to be handsome, cultured, well-versed in the court proceedings, able to converse with the king, and even advise him (Daniel was in a similar position. See Daniel 1:3-5). Such a position granted him considerable influence. He was there for "such a time as this" (See "Joint Op Intel" for week 1).

After four months of prayer and fasting for the rebuilding of Jerusalem, Nehemiah realized his part concerning the answer to his prayer. He knelt down to pray; then, he got up and began to work with resolution and grit. He courageously presented his request before the king, a request that could have cost his life. With the king's favor and permission, Nehemiah traveled to Jerusalem to rebuild the wall.

God Works in Us and Through Us

A journey of a thousand miles starts with one step. However, that first step sometimes prove to be the hardest. The task may seem impossible, but we do not rely on our strengths and abilities. We trust in a God who equips before he sends.

WEEK 1

MISSION DEBRIEF

DAY 1
How Did We Get Here?

DAY 2
Kneel Down to *Rise Up*

DAY 3
Marching Orders

DAY 4
Meet the OPFOR (Opposition Forces)

DAY 5
Boots on the Ground

JOINT OP INTEL
ESTHER: ADVOCATE FOR GOD'S PEOPLE
by Kelli Baker

H2O: PRAYER
by Melissa Hicks

How Did We Get Here?

1 and 2 Chronicles

BEFORE WE START, YOU MIGHT BE THINKING, "WAIT A SECOND! Do I need to read all of 1 and 2 Chronicles? I thought this was a study of Nehemiah. I want my money back!" No worry, friend. We need to do a *very quick* overview of history in order to understand the context of the story of Nehemiah. Without historical facts, we will misunderstand Nehemiah's drive to rebuild the wall. So, stick with me, it will be worth your time.

WHAT IS A COVENANT?

"A covenant is a chosen relationship or partnership in which two parties make binding promises to each other and work together to reach a common goal. Covenants are often accompanied by oaths, signatures, and ceremonies. They contain defined obligations and commitments but differ from a contract in that they are relational and personal. Think of a marriage. In love, a husband and wife choose to enter into a formal relationship binding themselves to one another in lifelong faithfulness and devotion. They then work as partners to reach a common goal, like building a career or raising children together. That's a covenant."

https://bibleproject.com/blog/covenants-the-backbone-bible/

Jerusalem had remained in ruins for almost a century. What happened to God's chosen people? Did he forsake them? How did they end up being taken into slavery?

Many commentators believe the writer of Nehemiah also wrote 1 and 2 Chronicles. Those two books give us a quick historical overview of Israel's history, starting with King David's reign. Let's gather some intel on what went wrong.

The first nine chapters of 1 Chronicles are genealogy. Chapter 10 introduces us briefly to Saul (Israel's first king) and King David. Chapters 10-16 focus on David's reign. Let's pick up after that.

MISSION DEBRIEF

1. Read 1 Chronicles 17:11-14. What was God's covenant with David? _____

    _____

    _____

    _____

    _____

2. Read 1 Chronicles 29:28. What does the writer say about David when he died?_____

    _____

    _____

    _____

    _____

3. The line of David begins with Solomon and ends with Zedekiah. As with any history, Israel had some good kings and some bad kings. Let's highlight a few.

Verses	Name of the King	Good or Evil?	Action Mentioned
2 Chronicles 12:13-14	Rehoboam	Evil	Did not seek the Lord
2 Chronicles 14:2-4			
2 Chronicles 17:3-5			
2 Chronicles 21:6-7			
2 Chronicles 24:20-22			
2 Chronicles 28:1-4 (Fall of Judah)			
2 Chronicles 36:5-6 (beginning of the exile)			

God demonstrated great patience with his people. Many centuries passed (over 400 years) before Jerusalem fell into the hands of the Babylonians, taking the Jews captive. Yet God's promise to David remained and later fulfilled in Jesus (Matthew 1:1). In the meantime, the exiles rested on a promise uttered by the prophet Jeremiah.

4.   Read Jeremiah 29:10-12. What hope did God promise his people in these verses? _____

_____

_____

_____

_____

5.   Have you experienced hard times that were linked to your own poor choices? List them here

and reflect upon how God can use them for your benefit. _____

_____

_____

_____

_____

The Bible says that God is slow to anger, compassionate, and steadfast in love. He allowed tough times to fall on Israel to bring his people back to him. Redemption and reconciliation are the driving forces of the divine mission. Along the way, God looks for people whose hearts seek him—who willing choose to join the ranks and fight the good fight. We will discover that Nehemiah was such a person.

DEEP DIVE

Face-Off: Solomon in light of Deuteronomy 17

If you are at all familiar with King Solomon, it might be because of his mother (Bathsheba), or his wisdom (the Book of Proverbs is attributed to him), or his wealth. Though Solomon is well known for his wisdom, his disregard for God's commandments prompted Israel's downfall.

Read the 2 Chronicles passages listed and write out what Solomon did. In the other column look up the Deuteronomy verses and list what God's command was.

MISSION DEBRIEF

Verses	Solomon's actions	God's Commands
2 Chronicles 9:25, 28 Deuteronomy 17:16		
2 Chronicles 9:24, 27 Deuteronomy 17:17b		
1 Kings 11:3 Deuteronomy 17:17a		

Sadly, Solomon turned away from God when the riches of the world appeared more enticing. It's easy to point fingers, but any of us can be led astray. As Christians, we no longer live under the law, but under grace. But that is not a carte blanche to do whatever we choose (Romans 6:1-2). What can lead us astray? Let me share ways I have failed God. Maybe you can relate:

- Following my heart, instead of following God's Word.
- Wallowing in deep hurts that make me think God has failed me.
- Focusing on being popular, instead of being a servant leader.
- Looking for love in the wrong places.

What would you place on your list? Naturally, we conform to the world, because we live in the world. But God holds better plans for us.

I encourage you to turn Romans 12:2 into a daily commitment to not conform to the world, but be transformed by the renewal of your mind to discern God's will.

DAY 2

Kneel Down to Rise Up

HAVE YOU EVER BEEN TEMPTED TO IDENTIFY A PROBLEM AND jump into action? Reed Bonadonna talks about this in his book, *How to Think like an Officer*. "Experience had taught me…that before rushing into action, it is advisable to get quite clearly fixed in the mind what the object of it all should be."[1]

Certain instances require immediate actions – like when a grenade falls into your bunker. In other circumstances rushing can lead to mistakes – like marrying the guy you just met. Our first response needs to be prayer. We need to turn to God for counsel. I have personally been strengthened when I ceased striving and acknowledged God for who he is (Psalm 46:10).

> "Do not be rash with your mouth, nor let your heart be hasty to utter a word before God, for God is in heaven, and you are on earth. Therefore, let your words be few" (Ecclesiastes 5:2). This wise counsel in the Book of Ecclesiastes reminds us that God's holy and righteous character should be the backbone of our prayers. When I remember God's character, humility fuels my prayers with the conviction that God is faithful, trustworthy, and in control. Humility becomes essential. Consider James 4:10, "Humble yourselves before the Lord, and he will exalt you."

1. Read Nehemiah 1:5. How did Nehemiah the beginning of his prayer demonstrate humility?_

   _____

   _____

   _____

   _____

---

1 Think like an Officer by Reed Bonadonna Stackpole Books ⊠ 2020 page 45

MISSION DEBRIEF

2.   Nehemiah trusted God's character. What do the following verses reveal about God's character?

Verses	God's character
Exodus 34:6-7	
Exodus 20:6	
Joel 2:13	

3.   How can those truths fortify your trust in God? _____

_____

_____

_____

_____

4.   Read Nehemiah 1:6-8. Nehemiah began by acknowledging God's character, then he moved to an essential aspect of the prayer. What is it? _____

_____

_____

_____

_____

5.   Compare Nehemiah's prayer in this passage (Nehemiah 1:6-8) to Leviticus 26:14-15, 33. What do you notice about his prayer? _____

_____

_____

_____

_____

MISSION DEBRIEF

6.   Nehemiah acknowledged God, confessed his sins, and was then ready to present his requests to God. Read Nehemiah 1:8-11. What is he asking?_____

_____

_____

_____

_____

This beautiful prayer in Nehemiah is still used today by modern-day Jews. It shows the importance of knowing God, his character, and his promises. It also instills hope of God's faithfulness to those who humble themselves and seek him with all their hearts.

Consider using Nehemiah's prayer as a template to write your own.

DEEP DIVE

1.   Read Daniel 9:3-19. What similarities can found in Daniel's prayer and Nehemiah's prayer?

_____

_____

_____

_____

2.   Read Leviticus 26:39-45 and Deuteronomy 4:29-31. What promises did Nehemiah recall in his prayer? _____

_____

_____

_____

_____

DAY 3

Marching Orders

Read Nehemiah 2:1-8.

"**T**HIS IS ABOVE MY PAY GRADE." HAVE YOU EVER USED THAT expression? It can suggest that you might not be qualified for the job.

My friend Kelli found herself in that type of situation. While stationed at Fort Bragg, her Psychological Operation Unit deployed downrange. A few months prior, Kelli's team leader got into some trouble, and she found herself in charge of the team. The added responsibilities, compounded by the heightened fear of deployment, felt heavy on her shoulders. She shared, "During this time, I was stretched beyond my limits. Immersed in a leadership position without the proper rank on my chest required even more work on my part, but I knew the Lord was with me."

"If God is for you, who can stand against you?" (Romans 8:31).

Strengthened by four months of prayer and fasting, Nehemiah is ready to approach the king.

"Then the king said to me, 'what are you requesting?'" Nehemiah 2:4.

1.   Read Nehemiah 2:5, 7-8a. What was Nehemiah's request? _____

_____

_____

_____

_____

MISSION DEBRIEF

2. Read Nehemiah 2:8b. How does the King's answer demonstrate God's favor on Nehemiah?

    _____

    _____

    _____

    _____

    King Artaxerxes liked and trusted Nehemiah. This speaks volumes about our hero's integrity and character.

Sidenote: Some Jewish commentators suggest the queen mentioned in verse six is none other than Queen Esther, Artaxerxes' mom. (See Joint Op Intel on Esther).

    This passage in Nehemiah speaks about two critical concepts: divine providence and human responsibility. God never stops working and uses his people to fulfill the mission. Others before Nehemiah had heard God's call and rose to the occasion:

*   Noah built an ark (which technically makes the first navy ever established).
*   Abraham left his homeland to pursue a promise.
*   Moses freed a people from slavery.

3. Read Esther 4:14. Haman is persecuting the Jews. The situation escalated to a critical point, and they face extermination. What does Mordecai's plead? _____

    _____

    _____

    _____

    _____

Esther took responsibility, risked her life, and saved the Jews. We all have a choice. When the time comes, when the marching orders are written, when God puts a burden on our heart -- the ball is then in our court, and we can rise to the occasion or not.

MISSION DEBRIEF

4. Are you sensing God's call for you in this season of your life? Describe it._____

    _____

    _____

    _____

    _____

5. Read Matthew 4:18-20. What marching orders does Jesus give his disciples? _____

    _____

    _____

    _____

    _____

Believing and doing go hand in hand. Faith says, "I'm all in" and propels us into action. A living faith entails an active faith.

"But be doers of the word, and not hearers only, deceiving yourselves" (James 1:22).

DEEP DIVE

We often hear the phrase "follower of Jesus," but what does it mean to be his disciple? Simply put, it means we reorganize our lives around three goals:

- To be with Jesus (prayer, solitude, Bible study).
- To become like Jesus (abiding in him will develop the fruit of the Spirit[2] in our lives).
- To do what Jesus did (face injustice, heal people, share the Word, fellowship with others).

Read John 8:31-32. What gift comes from being a disciple of Jesus?_____

_____

_____

_____

_____

---

2 Galatians 5:22-23

MISSION DEBRIEF

The word discipline may invoke thoughts of constraint and hardship. Jesus tells us the opposite. When we discipline ourselves to follow him, we not only learn the truth, but we are set free. I pray you will hear "follow me," step into action, and experience the abundant life promised by God (John 10:10).

DAY 4

Meet the OPFOR (Opposition Forces)

Read Nehemiah 2:10.

"**JUST AS WE DEVELOP OUR PHYSICAL MUSCLES THROUGH** overcoming opposition - like lifting weights - we develop our character muscles by overcoming challenges and adversity" (Stephen Covey[3]).

Wouldn't it be nice to live in a world where perfection reigns? Sounds like Utopia, right? Reality proclaims that opposition to worthwhile endeavors should be expected. Hard times develop our character as we grow through experience.

As soon as Nehemiah arrived in Jerusalem, he met the story's villains: Sanballat and Tobiah.

1. Read Nehemiah 2:10. What do we learn about these two characters? _____

    _____

    _____

    _____

    _____

2. Why do you think they were opposed to the welfare of Jerusalem? _____

    _____

    _____

    _____

    _____

---

3 *Stephen R. Covey, A. Roger Merrill, Rebecca R. Merrill (1997). "First Things First Every Day: Daily Reflections- Because Where You're Headed Is More Important Than How Fast You Get There", p.115, Simon and Schuster*

3. Read John 16:33. Should we be surprised when we face hard times? What promise can we take to heart? _____

    _____

    _____

    _____

    _____

4. Are you facing hard times? What would it look like for you to hang on to Jesus' promise? ___

    _____

    _____

    _____

    _____

We encounter Sanballat and Tobiah several times during our study of Nehemiah. They had a disdain for the Israelites. Nehemiah responded to their opposition with a prayer. Instead of retaliating, he trusted in God. I am often encouraged and empowered, knowing that Jesus has already overcome the world. Opposition will come, but I have hope.

DEEP DIVE

Read XYZ

The beautiful young queen, known as Esther, saved the Jews from grave danger. Using skilled diplomacy and sharp discernment, she revealed Haman's plot and secured a posh position for Mordecai in the king's court.

MISSION DEBRIEF

1. Read Esther 4:15-17. What crucial thing did she accomplish before stepping into action? ____

   _____

   _____

   _____

   _____

   Prayer, humbling ourselves, and seeking God should always be our first response when facing tough times. When attacked the temptation allures us to respond tit-for-tat. God teaches us a different way.

2. Does your current situation require action? Please write your prayer here. _____

   _____

   _____

   _____

   _____

DAY 5

MISSION DEBRIEF

Boots on The Ground

Read Nehemiah 2:9-20.

MILITARY ACTION CAN MEAN MANY THINGS. AIRSTRIKES ARE often first, but there comes a time that warrants face-to-face confrontation. Those times call for "boots on the ground".

Nehemiah knew he had to be present and fully involved in the project to rebuild the wall. As soon as he received the king's blessing, he traveled to Jerusalem. Nine hundred miles away, this journey would have taken many months.

1.   Read Nehemiah 2:11. What do you think Nehemiah did during the three days? _____

_____

_____

_____

_____

2.   Resting stands as an essential and sometimes overlooked part of leadership. We cannot properly serve when exhaustion overwhelms us. What did Jesus invite his disciples to do in Mark 6:31?_____

_____

_____

_____

MISSION DEBRIEF

3. Read Nehemiah 2:11-16. Why do you think Nehemiah did not want anyone to know his actions? (Consider the opposition facing him.)_____

_____

_____

_____

_____

Not merely relying on what his brother (Nehemiah 1:1-3) shared with him, Nehemiah was making his own observations. He realized the potential, and he willingly faced the problem.

The stage is set. Let us rise up and build! (Nehemiah 2:18)

4. What is God calling you to build in this season of your life? How can you rise up? _____

_____

_____

_____

_____

DEEP DIVE

Read Psalm 19.

The Psalms often reflect the feelings and emotions of the person writing. Psalm 19 has 14 verses reflecting on the beauty of God's Word and why it needs to be our foundation.

From what we know about Nehemiah, we can deduce that he was a man of the Word, a man seeking God before taking the next step.

MISSION DEBRIEF

1. Read Psalm 19:7-9. One should always read and meditate on God's Word. What benefits does this passage list? _____

    _____

    _____

    _____

    _____

2. Read verse 14. How does praying this verse change your attitude, your thoughts, and your actions? _____

    _____

    _____

    _____

    _____

    Adversity matures our character, and an upright character emerges when God is our compass.

Congratulations! You have finished week one of this study. Take time to pause and reflect on the lessons learned. I hope that you are encouraged by Nehemiah and realize that the call to rise up stands for all of us.

Esther: Advocate For God's People

By Kelli Baker

Like Nehemiah, Esther advocated for the Jewish people. An orphan raised by her cousin Mordecai, Esther found herself in a unique position. King Xerxes of Persia, after furiously throwing the current queen off her throne, began a search for a replacement. Esther was given the opportunity to become queen. When the time came to present herself to the king, she exemplified bravery as she stood before him. She concealed her true identity in hopes of winning the king's favor. "She won grace and favor" in the sight of the king (Esther 2:17). The king was captivated by her beauty and immediately chose her. Esther sought to glorify God in all that she did rather than use her beauty for her own glory.

Esther furthered her influence and favor with the king after saving his life. When Mordecai revealed to her that two guards were conspiring to assassinate the king, she immediately disclosed this to King Xerxes. Esther was strategic in her approach to the king, careful to give credit to Mordecai where credit was due. She knew how to approach the king with her requests without coming across as needy or obnoxious. As wives and Christian women in uniform, we must be cautious of how we interact with others. This very fine line is what women in uniform must walk as they navigate leadership in the military. Coming across as too aggressive can be misconstrued as mean or hostile; a more passive approach can be misconstrued as weak or incompetent.

As leaders, we must discern the call God has given us and learn how to communicate effectively to fulfill his call in all areas of our lives.

Esther became King Xerxes' greatest treasure because of her loyalty to him, and he sought to fulfill all of her requests. Haman, the king's second in command, demanded that Mordecai bow down to him; but Mordecai was faithful to God and did not comply. Infuriated, Haman devised a plan to kill Mordecai and all the Jews in the land. Mordecai revealed this plan to Esther and explained to her that saving the Jewish people might be her life's calling.

"And who knows whether you have not come to the kingdom for such a time as this?" (Esther 4:14b).

She immediately called for all the Jews to fast and pray, much like Nehemiah did prior to requesting permission from his king to build the wall. Rather than run away in fear, Esther boldly came before the king and requested that Haman be executed for his decree against the Jews.

She rose up for her people.

When God calls us to fulfill his will, it can often be daunting. This propels true faith into play in our lives. Jesus says in 2 Corinthians 12:9, "My grace is sufficient for you for my power is made perfect in weakness."

As Christian military women, we can learn God's will for us by using Esther's example as a guide. She fasted and prayed to receive guidance on how to move forward with the king. We can fast and pray when it comes time to request a special need or concern, such as our next duty assignment.

God will use our times of fasting and prayer to reveal himself to us. The Lord has already called you, and he will see you through, just as he did with Nehemiah and Esther.

Prayer

Habits to Outcome

By Melissa Hicks

> *I love the LORD, because he has heard my voice and my pleas for mercy. Because he inclined his ear to me, therefore I will call on him as long as I live. I will offer to you the sacrifice of thanksgiving and call on the name of the LORD. (Psalm 116:1-2, 17)*

We've seen this week that Nehemiah was clearly a man of prayer. Sometimes he prayed intermittently, while at other times he spent months in prayer. As we seek to become women who can *rise up to the call.* We need to be women who don't just pray before meals, or when we wake up in the morning, but women who pray without ceasing, women who spend extensive time with our heavenly Father.

We all find ourselves at different stages in our ever evolving praying life. Find here some practical ways to weave prayer throughout your day (1 Thessalonians 5:17). Depending on where you are in your prayer life, choose one of the following to challenge yourself in this area:

- Pray during mindless tasks, such as washing dishes or folding laundry.
- Set an alarm on your phone as a reminder to pray.
- Place sticky note reminders/requests in visible places (the bathroom mirror, the refrigerator, and more).
- Link social media to prayer: every time you open it and see the first post, pray for that person.
- Use personal cues for the people in your life. For example, when you see the color red, pray for the person whose favorite color is red.
- Pray during PT (Physical Training).

H₂0

BONUS: HOW TO CREATE A MINI PRAYER RETREAT (NEHEMIAH 1:4)

- Schedule it. A day of prayer won't happen without intentionality. Set a date and find a quiet location.

- Gather supplies: Bible, notebook, pen or pencil, a way to keep track of time, additional resources, such as prayer lists from your church or chapel, devotional books on prayer, memory verse cards, or a hymnbook.

- Find a quiet place where you won't be interrupted.

- Break the day into 3 parts:

  1. **Wait on God** – Experience his presence (read Psalm 139), ask God to search your heart (read Psalm 51 or 32), and worship him (Read Psalms 103, 111, 145, and Revelation 4 and 5).

  2. **Pray for Others** – Ask specific things for them, imagining yourself in their situation. Pray some of the prayers in Scripture (Philippians 1, Colossians 1, Ephesians 3). Pray for others what you pray for yourself.

  3. **Pray for Yourself** – Ask for understanding of the Scriptures (Psalm 119:18). Bring up problems, turning points, or decisions. List the factors involved, and pray over them, looking to the Bible for direction.

Keep things varied. Read, walk around, pray, sing. If you want to enhance things even further, consider fasting throughout your day of prayer.

References
___

Wendy Pope, "Creative Reminders to Pray," Proverbs 31 Ministries Devotions, accessed 7/6/2020, https://proverbs31.org/read/devotions/full-post/2014/02/11/creative-reminders-to-pray

Encourage your Spouse, "23 Easy Ways to Remember to Pray," Encourage your Spouse, accessed 7/6/2020, https://encourageyourspouse.com/23-easy-ways-to-remember-to-pray/

Lorne C. Sanny, "How to Spend a Day in Prayer" in *Deepening your Roots in God's Family,* ed. Ron Oertli (Colorado Springs, CO: NavPress, 2011), p. 94-101.

WEEK 2
Rise Up Against Oppression

"When my country, into which I had just set my foot, was set on fire about my ears, it was time to stir. It was time for every man to stir."

—THOMAS PAINE[4]

DECEMBER 1777—VALLEY FORGE. SIX DAYS BEFORE CHRISTMAS, a weary Continental Army led by George Washington arrived at Valley Forge. The men were hungry and tired after losing several battles. The British military occupied Philadelphia, our capital at the time. George Washington was facing two fronts—the British, who seemed to be winning, and the Continental Congress, who believed he was incompetent.

The winter was harsh, and the losses were heavy. Two thousand men died of hunger and disease. Friedrich Wilhelm Baron von Steuben, a Prussian officer, arrived in Valley Forge. George Washington, impressed by his countenance, appointed him Inspector General. Baron von Steuben enforced standards and drilled the troops tirelessly. Soldiers built and reinforced the camp. By June 1778, they emerged well-trained and rejuvenated. It was a turning point in the War for Independence. The winter of 1777-78 marked the birth of the American army.

Oppressed on two fronts, George Washington was fueled by his deep convictions and accomplished his mission. He did not succumb to oppression but rose up against it. The support he received from fellow soldiers was instrumental in that success.

With a Little Help from My Friends

As we continue our study of Nehemiah, we will observe how Nehemiah handled the strong opposition he faced. Upon arriving in Jerusalem, he confronted the harsh reality of a fallen city. Even

---

4 Common Sense by Thomas Paine p. 25 Penguin Books

though he was fully confident in his calling and demonstrated great faith in God, he would not have accomplished much without dedicated supporters.

I'm sometimes reluctant to ask for help. Often it is because I don't want to bother anybody. And sometimes my pride kicks in – "I can do this alone." It rarely takes me long to realize the idiocy of my thinking. Created to live in community, we are not lone rangers. We all need partners for the journey.

Friends or Foe

"The Bible tells us to love our neighbors, and also to love our enemies; probably because generally they are the same people." G.K. Chesterson[5]

Rebuilding and repairing Jerusalem meant a change was coming. Things would look different, which would disturb some who had taken advantage of a weakened population. Nehemiah had a single focus – the glory of God. For him, repairing the wall meant restoring a fallen nation – God's people. "Let us rebuild the wall of Jerusalem, that we may no longer suffer derision" (Nehemiah 2:17), The surrounding nations had been mocking them for years. The mocking continued even as they were tirelessly working: "What are these feeble Jews doing?" (Nehemiah 4:2) Since the Jews were God's chosen people, their enemies were not simply making fun of them, they were defying God. This did not sit well with our protagonist.

Ridicule, teasing, and contempt can take a toll on our determination. Bullies tend to attack when they feel threatened, or they and are jealous of our accomplishments. I remember being bullied in school, and I wish this type of harassment had stayed on the school playground. But being a Christian does not make us immune to mocking and opposition. As soon as we set our mind to do God's work, we will surely encounter opposition.

The Real Enemy

"We do not wrestle against flesh and blood, but against the rulers, against the authorities, against the cosmic powers over this present darkness, against the spiritual forces of evil in the heavenly places" (Ephesians 6:12).

---

5 The Soul of the Earth by Samuel A. Nigro, MD p. 117

The villains of our story have names: Sanballat, Tobiah, the Ammonites, the Ashdodites. Nehemiah never responded to their threats and taunts. Instead, he turned to God. "Hear, O our God, for we are despised" (Nehemiah 4:4). The enemies may have a name, but the spiritual forces behind them are the targets of Nehemiah's prayer. God was his first course of action, because he understood where the real battle took place.

We, too, do not wrestle against flesh and blood, but against the spiritual forces of evil.

Armed with the proper weapons (both spiritual and physical), Nehemiah completed the wall (its dimensions are 2½ miles and 39 feet high) in 52 days. Quite an achievement, especially since he faced such persistent and significant opposition.

This is our reality as well. When we build, we will battle. Armed with the proper mindset, we too can rise up and prevail against oppression.

WEEK 2

MISSION DEBRIEF

DAY 1

DAY 2

DAY 3

DAY 4

DAY 5

JOINT OP INTEL

H2O

DAY 1

Lead from The Front

Read Nehemiah 3.

REBUILDING THE WALL WAS A TREMENDOUS TASK. IT WAS NOT going to happen overnight, and it needed careful planning. As you read through Nehemiah 3, you will notice the organization and coordination that went into the effort. Nehemiah had a plan—and he worked his plan.

Leaders can set the example by joining in the work themselves. Leading from the front means that you are taking an active part in the mission. The high priest was a leader in the Jewish community, and he was actively participating (Nehemiah 3:1). But he was not alone.

1. Look at verses 2, 5, 7, 8, 12, 32 in Nehemiah chapter 3. How many people are mentioned? _

   _____

   _____

   _____

   _____

2. Times may change, but human nature stays the same. What does Nehemiah 3:5 highlight?___

   _____

   _____

   _____

   _____

MISSION DEBRIEF

3. Most people worked, a few did not, and some worked more (see Nehemiah 3:11, 19, 21, 24, 27, 30). We can easily get distracted by what is going on around us. We can be discouraged by insufficient participation. _____

_____

_____

_____

4. Read Philippians 3:12-14. What encouragement and directive does Paul provide in these verses? How can you apply his example in your life and set a standard for others? _____

_____

_____

_____

I love the picture drawn in Nehemiah 3 of people standing next to each other, repairing a part of the wall. This chapter starts at the Sheep Gate and ends at the Sheep Gate. Workers from different backgrounds, united by a common goal, worked together to repair the wall from start to finish. What a beautiful picture of community. Everyone was welcome to work, and everybody had a place at the wall.

DEEP DIVE

Many Gifts – One Body

Have you ever stubbed your toe? Or smashed your thumb? Although only one part of your body is injured, the rest feels the pain. Intellectually, we are well aware that the hand does not have the same function as the mouth, and that the leg does not copy the stomach's behavior. Each part of the body has a distinct role, so the body can function as one.

MISSION DEBRIEF

The Church is often referred to as a body. As members of the body, we have different functions depending on the gifts/talents God has given us.

1. Read 1 Corinthians 12:4-11. How many spiritual gifts are listed?

Verse	Spiritual Gift
v.8	wisdom
v.8	
v.9	
v.9	
v.10	
v.10	
v.10	
v.10	
v.10	

2. According to the same verses, who empowers those gifts in us?_____

_____

_____

_____

_____

3. Read 1 Corinthians 12:7 again. What is the purpose of the gifts we have been given?_____

_____

_____

_____

_____

MISSION DEBRIEF

4.   Read 1 Corinthians 12:14-20. According to this passage, are some gifts better than others?

What would happen if we decided that our gift is useless? _____

_____

_____

_____

_____

What are your gifts? What can you do today to use your gifts? Do you believe that you too have a place at the wall? If you do not know your spiritual gift you can take an assessment either online (www. spiritualgiftstest.com) or in person. Discuss your results with a mature Christian friend.[6]

Nehemiah needed all "boots on the ground" to rebuild the wall. It did not matter if they were priests, carpenters, jewelers, men or women. What mattered was that they were willing to stand elbow-to-elbow and rebuild together.

---

6 If you don't know your spiritual gift, there are lots of spiritual gift assessments available free online.

DAY 2

Fake News

Read Nehemiah 4:1-6.

THE MAIN PURPOSE OF FAKE NEWS (ALSO KNOWN AS JUNK NEWS, pseudo-news, alternative facts, or hoax) is to undermine, disinform, and mislead. Are you grounded in your true identity with God? Are you equipped and ready to face the weapons of the enemy? Only then can you isolate the lie and stand with the truth. Fake news did not originate through modern-day campaigns of disinformation. It all began with a devious question uttered in the Garden of Eden: "Did God really say . . .?"[7]

Did you skim over the list of names in Nehemiah 3? I tend to do that as well. There are many Bible passages with long lists of names and genealogies with no end in sight. They are hard to pronounce and seem to bring no value to the passage.

When you walk into a military headquarters, you will likely see a wall with a brief history of that unit and a few heroes' names. Proud of their heritage, Soldiers, Sailors, Airmen, and Marines value those who have come before them. Their names are part of the unit's identity. The genealogies in Nehemiah serve the same purpose, linking the people to their past with the reminder of their heritage.

"Ridicule is the language of the devil," - Thomas Carlyle[8].

It is not out of character for the enemy to insult God's workers. It is a tactic that targets our identity. Rarely a blatant lie, it is usually a half-truth. Let's look at a few examples.

---

7 Genesis 3:1
8 *Sartor Resartus* published in Frasers Magazine 1833

MISSION DEBRIEF

1. Read Nehemiah 4:2-3. What are Sanballat and Tobiah saying about the Jews? _____

    _____

    _____

    _____

    _____

2. Read 1 Samuel 17:41-47. How did Goliath start the battle? _____

    _____

    _____

    _____

3. During the crucifixion, Jesus suffered tremendous physical pain. However, the abuse was not just physical. Read Luke 22:63-65 and Luke 23:35-37. What weapon was used against him?_

    _____

    _____

    _____

    _____

4. Many heroes of the faith endured mocking (Hebrews 11:36). Ridicule can hurt us, but the words of an enemy can only poison us when we spend time pondering them. The antidote is standing firm on the truth that God speaks over us. _____

    _____

    _____

    _____

    _____

MISSION DEBRIEF

5.   Here are some of the things that God says about you. Match each verse to its truth.

Genesis 1:27   More valuable than sparrows
Psalm 139:14   Created in God's image
Matthew 10:30   Knit together in my mother's womb
Psalm 139:13   Fearfully and wonderfully made
Matthew 10:31   He knows how many hairs on my head
1 Peter 1:3   Loved by a perfect Father
Ephesians 1:5   Born again to a new identity
1 John 3:1   Adopted into God's family

6.   Which verses remind you of God's truth about you?_____

_____

_____

_____

_____

Nehemiah was confident in his identity as one of God's chosen people. The names of those helping him also belong to God. Their faith is firmly rooted in that identity. The Tekoites (Nehemiah 3:5), for example, produced the oil used in the temple. Hasshub, the son of Pahath-moab (Nehemiah 3:11) is a descendant of King David. The lists of names have purpose and meaning – they are a reminder of each servant's identity as God's chosen.

DEEP DIVE

The Power of The Truth

Do you know how people in Finland fight fake news? They use education. In Europe, Finland ranks first in media literacy, closely followed by Denmark and the Netherlands. They "teach children how to use doubt intelligently and to understand that uncertainty can be quantified and measured."[9]

9 https://www.weforum.org/agenda/2019/05/how-finland-is-fighting-fake-news-in-the-classroom/

MISSION DEBRIEF

The devil uses fake news in our lives as well. He rarely comes at us with a blatant lie, but with a half-truth, creating enough doubt in our mind to drive us to the wrong conclusion.

So how do we fight fake news? We fight fake news with the truth of God's Word.

1. Read Colossians 1:9-10. How do we walk in a manner worthy of God? _____

    _____

    _____

    _____

    _____

2. Spiritual wisdom sounds nice, but how can it be obtained? What does James 1:5 say about

    obtaining wisdom? _____

    _____

    _____

    _____

We combat fake news with the truth of God. Our personal relationship with Jesus and our faith in him (Colossians 1:3) give us direct access to his wisdom. Prayer is a weapon we always need to carry (see last week's H2O).

DAY 3

Fear Tactics

Read Nehemiah 4:7-13.

PSYCHOLOGICAL OPERATION UNITS (PSYOPS) HAVE A SPECIFIC purpose. They induce or reinforce behaviors that are favorable to American objectives. They "convey selected information and indicators to audiences to influence their emotions, motives, and objective reasoning, and ultimately the behavior of governments, organizations, groups, and individuals."[10] When used correctly, those tactics can save countless lives as they entice the enemy to stop fighting.

We studied yesterday one of the tactics used by the enemy: ridicule. I remember when my middle child would come home in tears because of other kids' mean comments. It pained me to see the hurt in his eyes. I also knew that there was nothing I could do to make it go away. I would encourage him to ignore them and, more important, never show that it bothered him. With time, they would stop.

Nehemiah stood firm and was not bothered by ridicule. In return, his enemies elevated their taunts and threats.

1. Read Nehemiah 4:8 and 4:11. What was being planned? _____

    _____

    _____

    _____

    _____

---

10 https://en.wikipedia.org/wiki/Psychological_operations_(United_States)

MISSION DEBRIEF

2. What reaction do you think the Jews had upon hearing this? _____

    _____

    _____

    _____

    _____

    Fear is crippling and contagious. It can paralyze you and keep you from doing the work you are called to do. In his inaugural address on March 4, 1933, President Franklin Roosevelt proclaimed to a hurting nation, "The only thing we have to fear is fear itself."

3. Can you demonstrate great faith and be fearful at the same time? What does Jesus say about

    that in Matthew 8:26? _____

    _____

    _____

    _____

    _____

4. What fears are you facing? List them and bring them to God in prayer. Allow him to calm

    the storms in your heart. _____

    _____

    _____

    _____

    _____

MISSION DEBRIEF

DEEP DIVE

Be courageous.

Joshua was Moses' second-in-command. When Moses died Joshua became the leader. After wandering the desert for 40 years, the Israelites were ready to take possession of the Promised Land. First, they had to conquer the people living there. Joshua did not journal his feelings at the time, but I assume he must have been a bit anxious and nervous about the upcoming battles and his new leadership position.

1. Read Joshua 1:9. What is the command? What is the promise? _____

    _____

    _____

    _____

    _____

2. Often Joshua 1:9 is quoted alone. I believe the preceding verses shed light on how we too can

    be strong and courageous. Read Joshua 1:7-8. What is Joshua encouraged to do? What is the

    source of his courage and his success? How can you apply this concept to your life? How can

    this help you find courage? _____

    _____

    _____

    _____

    _____

The Word of God is a counteragent to fear (check this week's H2O). The more we study it and the longer we meditate on it, the stronger we get and the less fear we experience.

DAY 4

Spiritual Warfare

Read Nehemiah 4:14.

"**L**IFE IS DIFFICULT."[11] SCOTT PECK STARTS HIS BOOK, *THE ROAD Less Traveled,* with this simple yet profound statement. His observation is not meant to be depressive, but it is a fact of life. Difficulties and disappointments are easier to manage if we expect them.

1. What warning does Jesus give in John 16:33? _____

   _____

   _____

   _____

   _____

2. Read Ephesians 6:12. Whom does Paul identify as the origin of our adversity? _____

   _____

   _____

   _____

   _____

If we think our struggle is with our annoying neighbor, our chain of command, or our duty station, we will be tempted to take actions that will ultimately be unsuccessful. There is a better alternative: We can identify the <u>true source</u> of our struggle, our real enemy.

---

11 The Road Less Traveled. 25th Anniversary Edition p.15

3.   Read John 8:44. What does Jesus say about the devil? _____

_____

_____

_____

_____

4.   What promise does Jesus give in John 8:31-32? _____

_____

_____

_____

_____

Life is complicated, and we will face opposition. But we are not alone; we are not unequipped. As we continue our study, we will appreciate how Nehemiah always prays first, then addresses the situation. This is the reason he gives God the glory in Nehemiah 4:14.

Identify the real enemy. Utilize the arsenal of weapons at your disposal (Ephesians 6:10-18, aka the armor of God) and be combat-ready at all times.

DEEP DIVE

The Armor of God. Ephesians 6:10-18

Winston Churchill once said, "The empires of the future are the empires of the mind."[12] Digital culture, art, and pop-culture shape our hearts and minds more than we realize. There is a concept called "mental maps." A "mental map is a person's point-of-view perception of their area of interaction."[13] It is how you see and understand the world around you. We all have them. Mental maps enable us to make coffee in the morning or get to work without much thought. We accomplish those habitual tasks without much thinking, because they are stored in our memory bank. When our mental maps

---

12 Winston Churchill, Speech at Harvard University, September 6, 1943.
13 https://en.wikipedia.org/wiki/Mental_mapping

are accurate, we get from point A to point B without any issues. When our mental maps are not accurate, our perception of reality is distorted.

Our mental maps direct our choices concerning relationships, work ethics, and parenting, to name a few. To perceive reality accurately, we need to be well-informed. God has given us the proper tools to enlighten us and equip us.

1. Read Ephesians 6:10-12. What reasons does Paul list for putting on the armor of God?_____

    _____

    _____

    _____

    _____

2. Read Ephesians 6:14-17. What are the different parts of the armor, and what is each one's

    purpose?

Verses	Part of the Armor	Purpose
v.14	belt	truth
v.14		
v.15		
v.16		
v.17		
v.17		

MISSION DEBRIEF

3. Pick two or three parts of the armor and write down where you can wield this weapon. _____

_____

_____

_____

_____

In the military, we do not wait for the enemy to show up before we train. We train constantly so that we are ready to fight when needed. In the spiritual realm, combat readiness means putting on the whole armor of God. These truths need to be written on our hearts:

- Strap on the belt of truth – know the Bible by diligently reading and studying it.

- Put on the breastplate of righteousness – We are a new creation in Christ, and his righteousness covers us.

- Slip on our gospel of peace shoes – Armed with the good news of Jesus, we are called to love.

- Always bring the shield of faith – God is for us and will fight for us.

- Do not forget the helmet of salvation – We are Christians saved by grace, and we belong to God's family.

- Last but not least, our offensive weapon, the sword of the spirit – God's Word (the Bible) is truth. The truth will eventually debunk every lie.

Is the Bible your GPS? Is God's truth the foundation for what you believe about the world? What will you do to ensure that your mental map is accurate?

DAY 5

Rally Point

Read Nehemiah 4:15-23.

DO YOU HAVE AN EMERGENCY PLAN? WITH EVERY PCS (Permanent Change of Station), our family emergency plan is revisited and revised. The kids are drilled on what to do in a fire, tornado, hurricane, earthquake, or other emergency. The most important part of each plan is the rally point.

The Army Ranger Handbook explains this term: "A rally point is a place designated by the leader where the unit moves to reassemble and reorganize... Soldiers must know which rally point to move to at each phase of the mission should they become separated from the unit. They must also know what actions are required there...."[14]

1. Read Nehemiah 4:15. What is happening after the attempted attacks? _____

   _____

   _____

   _____

   _____

2. Having learned from their experience, they returned to work armed and ready. What is happening in Nehemiah 4:16-17? _____

   _____

   _____

   _____

   _____

---

14 Army Ranger Handbook Ch.7 p.14

MISSION DEBRIEF

Nehemiah was ready at any point to rally the troops in case of an emergency.

3.   What reminder is Nehemiah giving the people in verse 20? _____

_____

_____

_____

_____

I love this picture of a trumpet rallying us to a place where God will fight for us. I do not know what is going on in your life right now. I do know that we all face harsh times and opposition at one point or another. It gives me great peace to know that I have a rally point in Jesus, and that God will fight for me.

4.   How can you make God your rally point during a difficult season? _____

_____

_____

_____

_____

DEEP DIVE

Read Psalm 85.

As we finish this week's study, I want to encourage you to read and pray through Psalm 85. Make this your rally point this week. Stay at his feet and be strengthened for the journey ahead.

MISSION DEBRIEF

1.   Read verses 1-3. What is the psalmist doing? _____

_____

_____

_____

_____

There is power in taking time to remember what God has already accomplished in our lives. Those times are faith builders.

2.   Read verses 4-7. What is the plea? _____

_____

_____

_____

_____

When life beats you down, there is one place that is safe and restorative. Run into the arms of Jesus. He wants to be your rally point. I have found no better place when I've faced difficult times.

Good job on finishing week two. Nehemiah has given us some great pointers on how to deal with opposition. Next week, we will see how opposition can sometimes be found in our own ranks.

Daniel: Fearless Servant of God

By Kelli Baker

As Christians, we will be confronted with opposition. When we follow God and walk in his will, the enemy becomes infuriated and seeks to destroy us. Daniel, much like Nehemiah, faced opposition.

His story began when King Nebuchadnezzar directed that his chief eunuch bring him strong, youthful men from Israel to serve him. They were taken from their homeland and held captive in Babylon. Upon their arrival, Daniel and his three friends were given new names (Daniel was named Belteshazzar), forced to learn the language and literature of their new country, and stripped of their heritage and identity.

While we will probably never face such extreme treatment, the enemy is constantly working, tempting us to doubt our identity. He places seeds of doubt that make us question the work we are doing. He reminds us of our past and tries to convince us that we are not good enough for God. Or he tries to make us forget our past, so we forget our heritage and even our identity.

Daniel and his friends were given the choice food that the king ate. The Babylonians thought this would help them grow strong and healthy. Daniel strongly opposed eating unclean food as it was against God's commands.

"But Daniel resolved that he would not defile himself with the king's food, or with the wine that he drank. Therefore he asked the chief of the eunuchs to allow him not to defile himself" (Daniel 1:8).

The chief eunuch did not think it was a good idea. He said that the king would have his head if Daniel and his friends were allowed this. Daniel persisted. He asked the chief to let them eat only vegetables and drink only water for ten days. The chief eunuch agreed.

At the end of the ten days, Daniel and his friends "were in better appearance and fatter in flesh than all the youths who ate the king's food" (Daniel 1:15). Due to their obedience, God strengthened them, making them more fit for the job. Daniel became a leader by standing firm in his convictions. This opened the door for others to excel as well.

This was not the end of the opposition Daniel faced. Blessed with God's favor and armed with wisdom from above, Daniel and his friends were appointed over the affairs of the province. Their success, however, infuriated the other officials and satraps, so they plotted against Daniel. They convinced the king to sign a decree that whoever prayed to anyone but the king must be thrown into the lion's den. Shortly after the decree was posted, Daniel was found praying in his home. The king reluctantly threw Daniel in with the lions.

The next morning, after no sleep, the king went back to the lion's den to check on Daniel.

"As he came near to the den where Daniel was, he cried out in a tone of anguish. The king declared to Daniel, "O Daniel, servant of the living God, has your God whom you serve continually been able to deliver you from the lions?" (Daniel 6:20).

Daniel proudly exclaimed that the Lord had shut the mouths of the lions because no blame could be found against God or the king. Daniel's faithfulness and trust in God led to the king declaring that all people in the land were to "fear the God of Daniel, for he is the living God enduring forever" (Daniel 6:26a).

God used Daniel, an exile in a foreign land, in ways unimaginable. Always faithful, Daniel was able to witness the power of God by defeating his opposition. And just like Nehemiah, Daniel was used by God to encourage the people around him.

Standing firm in his faith, Daniel showcased God's faithfulness to all believers.

Scripture Memorization

Habits to Outcome

By Melissa Hicks

When we face opposition, as Nehemiah did, we need an offensive weapon. The Bible says this weapon is the Word of God (Ephesians 6:16-17). We are fortunate to live in a time when we have access to the Bible in multiple formats. Why then should we memorize Scripture when we have it so readily available in print or on the Internet?

BENEFITS OF MEMORIZING SCRIPTURE:

- Spiritual power - The Holy Spirit can embed memorized Scripture in our hearts and bring it to our attention when we need it most to combat temptation, fear, or opposition.

- Strong faith – Memorizing reinforces the truth of God's word and strengthens our faith.

- Preparation for witnessing/counseling – Sometimes God will bring to our minds a verse that we've memorized, and it will be the turning point in a conversation with another person. It may even lead them to faith in Christ.

- God's guidance – When we need to make difficult decisions, the Holy Spirit can guide us by reminding us of Scripture we've memorized.

- Meditation – When you memorize Scripture, you can meditate on it anywhere and at any time. Whether driving to work, rocking a baby, waiting in line at the commissary, or eating in the mess hall—you can be blessed by the Word of God.

H$_2$O

BELOW ARE SOME TIPS TO HELP YOU START MEMORIZING TODAY:

- Pick a verse or a passage of Scripture. If you need a plan or suggestions, look up the Topical Memory System (https://verses.life/tms/) or Fighter Verses (https://fighterverses.com/the-verses/fighter-verses/).

- Several Bible memory apps can help you practice and prompt you to review. Suggested apps are *Fighter Verses, Remember Me Bible Memory, Bible Memory.*

- Set verses to music (*The Verses Project* or *Seeds Family Worship* have verses set to music for you).

- Memorize the reference and the first phrase as one unit and repeat the reference at the end.

- Doodle the verse.

- Write the first letter of each word of the verse on the inside of your wrist.

- Post the verse you're working on in a place where you'll routinely see it.

- Record yourself saying the verse and listen to it while you drive.

- Set up a specific time of day to practice and review, tying it to a daily routine.

- Find someone to hold you accountable.

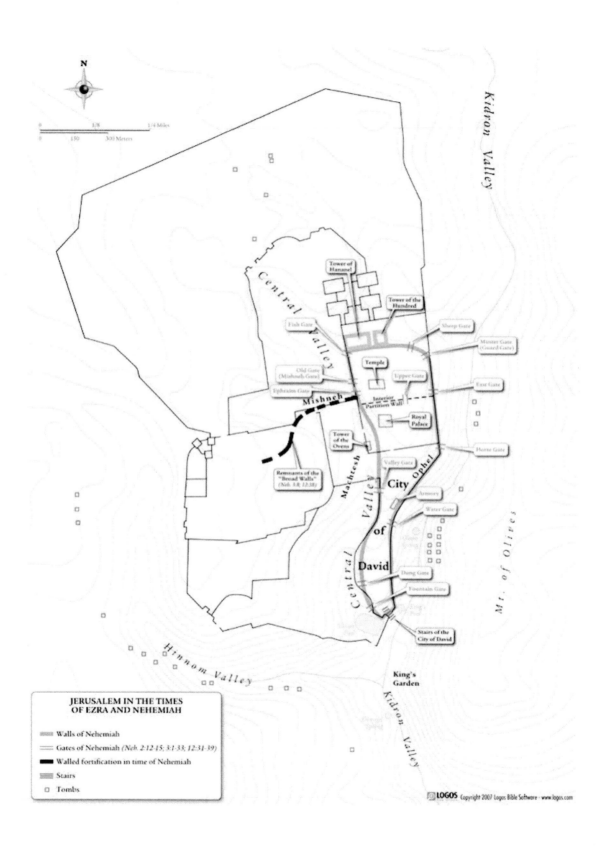

N

0   1/8   1/4 Miles
0   150   300 Meters

Kidron Valley

Central Valley

Tower of Hananel

Tower of the Hundred

Fish Gate

Sheep Gate

Muster Gate (Guard Gate)

Old Gate (Mishneh Gate)

Temple

Upper Gate

East Gate

Ephraim Gate

Mishneh

Interior Partition Wall

Royal Palace

Tower of the Ovens

Remnants of the "Broad Walls" *(Neh. 3:8; 12:38)*

Machtesh

Central Valley

Ophel

City

Valley Gate

Horse Gate

Armory

Water Gate

of

David

Dung Gate

Fountain Gate

Stairs of the City of David

Mt. of Olives

King's Garden

Kidron Valley

Hinnom Valley

JERUSALEM IN THE TIMES OF EZRA AND NEHEMIAH

Walls of Nehemiah

Gates of Nehemiah *(Neh. 2:12-15; 3:1-33; 12:31-39)*

Walled fortification in time of Nehemiah

Stairs

□ Tombs

Week 3
Rise Up for Justice

For sweetest things turn sourest by their deeds;
Lilies that fester smell far worse than weeds.

—*William Shakespeare*[15]

DECEMBER 1955—MONTGOMERY, ALABAMA. A YOUNG AFRICAN
American woman refuses to give up her seat on the bus. As a result, she is arrested and fined. Flyers circulate asking for a bus boycott on December 5, the day Rosa Parks was to appear in court. That afternoon, black leaders meet to form the Montgomery Improvement Association (MIA). They elect Dr. Martin Luther King, Jr. as their president. Their first call to action is to continue boycotting the buses until their requests are met. It will take 381 days, but their peaceful protest is successful.

Dr. King emerged as the leader of the civil rights movement. This event also solidified his commitment to non-violent resistance. He stayed true to his convictions until his assassination in 1968. An advocate of peaceful action, he penned these words in 1961, "In these turbulent days of uncertainty, the evils of war and economic and racial injustice threaten the very survival of the human race."[16] Those words still ring true today.

Moved by the injustice surrounding him, Dr. Martin Luther King, Jr. rose up and preached God's justice.

Sin is Crouching at Your Door

A great cry rose among the Jews. They were being oppressed, not by the Amorites, the Samaritans, or the Arabs. They were suffering at the hands of their own people. Jews exploiting Jews. Upon hearing about this injustice, Nehemiah didn't hesitate to take action.

---

15 Sonnet 94
16 Martin Luther King Jr. *Strength to Love* p. xiii

MISSION DEBRIEF

You are probably familiar with the expression "nip it in the bud." It means to suppress something at the early stages. Not doing anything about a sin we are aware of can lead to a stronghold[17]. When sin is crouching at our door, we need to address it instead of inviting it in or denying it even exists.

Backed by the Law of God, Nehemiah displayed holy anger against sin. He was unconcerned about what was popular. As a true leader, he stood for what was right, rather than what was safe.

The Enemy Within

"To consider persons and events and situations only in the light of their effect upon myself is to live on the doorstep of hell" - Thomas Merton.[18]

Nehemiah 5 and 6 reveal the depths of sin in the human heart and the importance of loving our neighbors as ourselves. Selfishness is the enemy within. Faced with deception and oppression, Nehemiah responded with spiritual discernment and integrity of character.

Rules of Engagement

Life provides us with plenty of opportunities to grow and learn. We may experience or witness injustice at work or in our social circle. Sometimes our response will not be popular. The Bible gives us clear directives on how to confront injustice in any situation in life. In the military, the term is "Rules of Engagement." It can be defined as follows, "The Rules of Engagement (ROE) are those directives that delineate the circumstances and limitations under which United States (US) forces will initiate and/or continue combat engagement."[19]

When we hear the call to rise up for justice, we first must learn and then apply the proper Rules of Engagement. Are you ready? Let's go!

---

17 Habitual pattern of thought, built into one's thought life
18 Warren W. Wiersbe *Be Determined* p.71
19 Law of War/ Introduction to Rules of Engagement B130936 Student handout p.2

WEEK 3

MISSION DEBRIEF

DAY 1

DAY 2

DAY 3

DAY 4

DAY 5

JOINT OP INTEL

H2O

Unraveling

Read Nehemiah 5:1-5.

THIS CHAPTER IN NEHEMIAH STANDS ALONE. IT IS AN INTERLUDE in the building of the wall. The pause was necessary in order to address issues that arose.

1. Read Nehemiah 5:1-4. Something is amiss. Some find the courage to speak up about their oppression. List the complaints mentioned by the people.

Verse	Complaint
1-2	
3	
4	

The poor were oppressed, and their cry was enough for Nehemiah to stop the work and address the situation. The people were hungry, and they were paying hefty taxes.

God is just and has always made provision for the poor, the widows, and the fatherless. He gave Moses specific laws on those topics.

MISSION DEBRIEF

2.   What does Leviticus 25:35-38 say regarding money lending? _____

_____

_____

_____

_____

3.   Read Deuteronomy 15:7-8. What does God ask concerning the treatment of the poor? _____

_____

_____

_____

_____

At the core of the issue is the sin of selfishness. When times are hard, it is tempting to look out for number one and forget the people around us. As Christians, we are to love God with all our hearts, minds, and souls, and love our neighbors as ourselves (Matthew 22:37-40). Christianity is about being selfless, not selfish.

4.   Read Philippians 2:1-8 and answer the following questions:

   a.   Whose example should we follow (v.5)? _____

   _____

   _____

   b.   How are we to treat others? _____

   _____

   _____

   c.   What character traits are highlighted in this passage? _____

   _____

   _____

MISSION DEBRIEF

How did Jesus react to injustice? When he was treated unjustly, he did not defend himself. However, when he witnessed injustice towards others, he reacted. He defended the poor, gave dignity to women, and spoke up for children.

5.   When we experience or witness injustice, how should we confront it? _____

_____

_____

_____

_____

It is not about me but about those around me. When I am self-focused, I may not notice people who are hurting. As Christians, we are called by God to take care of those in need and remain unstained from the world (James 1:27). When we see people suffering from injustice, we need to stand firmly on God's Word and speak up.

6.   Have you witnessed any inequities or wrongdoings? What can you do about it? _____

_____

_____

_____

_____

DEEP DIVE

Scandals of Biblical Proportion

Abuse of power, scandals, and mistreatment of people populate the news headlines and *Twitter* feeds. They are, however, not 21st century-breaking news. They are as old as time.

Let's explore a few.

MISSION DEBRIEF

Verses	Injustice Mentioned
Genesis 4:8-10	
Exodus 1:8-14	
2 Samuel 11:1-4	
2 Samuel 11:14-21	
2 Samuel 1-14	
Matthew 2:16	
Acts 7:54-60	

"Whoever oppresses a poor man insults his Maker" (Proverbs 14:31). God tells us how to rise up for justice.

1. Write out Isaiah 1:17._____

    _____

    _____

    _____

    _____

2. How can you apply this in your life?_____

    _____

    _____

    _____

DAY 2

Give Me Faith

Read Nehemiah 5:6-13

HAVE YOU EVER FOUND YOURSELF IN AN AWKWARD SOCIAL situation? Maybe it was an FRG (Family Readiness Group) meeting, and everybody was drinking. You would rather not, but you don't want to stand out. Has your chain of command ever done anything that contradicts your values? Do you go along with it? Or do you stay true to what you know is right?

Social psychologists refer to the term "mob" or "herd mentality" when expressing the concept of peer influence to adopt certain behaviors on a mostly emotional, rather than rational basis. After all, we are all just sheep (Ezekiel 34:31), and it is easy for us to be led astray.

We need discernment to recognize the voice of the Shepherd and follow his guidance.

1. Who is our Shepherd according to John 10:14? _____

    _____

    _____

    _____

    _____

2. Read John 10:27. What happens when we recognize the voice of the Shepherd?_____

    _____

    _____

    _____

    _____

MISSION DEBRIEF

Nehemiah never lost track of the purpose for his life and the voice he needed to follow. A wealthy man, he was also in a position of power. However, he did not side with his affluent peers.

3. How did Nehemiah react to the complaints of the people, according to Nehemiah 5:6-7?

    What actions did he take?_____

    _____

    _____

    _____

    _____

Anger is a tricky emotion. Paul reminds us not to sin in our anger (Ephesians 4:26). Nehemiah's indignation was righteous. He was angry because the people had disobeyed God's Word. Notice Nehemiah's first act: "I took counsel with myself," which means to ponder carefully. Not one to rush to decisions, Nehemiah took the time to gather all the intel and use discernment to make a wise decision.

4. The Bible has a lot of advice on being wise in our decision-making. Match each verse.

    Proverbs 2:6   Let God weigh your motives.

    Proverbs 3:5-6   Warning about being in haste with our decisions.

    Proverbs 16:2   True source of wisdom.

    Proverbs 18:13   Trust in God to make our paths straight.

    Proverbs 19:2   Take the time to listen before answering.

5. Maybe you are in a situation that calls for confrontation. Pray about it, and write down what your next step should be (confront in love, forgive, etc.). Are you ready to be bold and rise up for what is right? _____

_____

_____

_____

_____

Nehemiah's goal was restoration, not confrontation (see this week's H2O). We are to be peacemakers (Matthew 5:9). Maybe you can recall a time when someone voiced out loud what you were feeling inside. Did it empower you to join in with that person? Perhaps next time, you could be the first to speak up and empower somebody else.

Pray, seek God (James 1:5), listen to the shepherd's voice, and walk in his way.

DEEP DIVE

Biblical smackdown: Paul vs. Peter

Paul and Peter are giants of the faith. Jesus had appointed Peter to take care of his sheep—i.e., the Church (John 21:15-17). Peter walked with Jesus on this earth; Paul did not. Peter was there from the beginning; Paul joined in much later. Nevertheless, Peter's notoriety and high position within the church did not stop Paul from confronting him when it was necessary.

1. Read Galatians 2:11-14. What did Paul accuse Peter of?_____

_____

_____

_____

MISSION DEBRIEF

2. Why do you suppose Peter was acting that way? _____

_____

_____

_____

_____

It is not always easy to do what is right and stand for what is true. Maybe you are like me—a people pleaser—and you shy away from confrontation.

We cannot please men and please God (Galatians 1:10). Paul recognized that Peter's behavior contradicted what he claimed (Acts 10:34-35). Paul did not confront Peter to embarrass him, but to allow the truth of the gospel to shine forth.

I pray that you and I can be as bold as Paul and Nehemiah and speak the truth in love.

DAY 3

God Says – I Do

Read Nehemiah 5:14-19

HAVE YOU EVER WITNESSED A THREE-YEAR-OLD APOLOGIZING? My boys were…well boys, and a handful to manage at times. Often, I would have them apologize for their misdeeds. And they would. "I'm sorry." The words would come out of their mouths—but the tight lips, the annoyed look, and the arched back sent another message. What is cute and funny in a three-year old is hurtful and hypocritical in an adult. How does 1 John 3:18 speak to the truth that mere words are not enough?

HYPOCRISY

Noun: the practice of claiming to have moral standards or beliefs to which one's own behavior does not conform; pretense.

1. The Bible has a lot to say about hypocrisy. What do the following verses warn us about?

Verses	Warning
Titus 1:16	
Matthew 15:7-9	
James 1:22-23	
Matthew 23:23	

Yesterday, we read about Nehemiah's confrontation. He was part of a wealthy community, and he was a man of power. What is remarkable about him is that he used his influence to set a great example.

66

MISSION DEBRIEF

2.   Read Nehemiah 5:14-15. What did Nehemiah choose not to do? What was his motivation? _

_____

_____

_____

_____

3.   What decision is listed in Nehemiah 5:16? _____

_____

_____

_____

_____

4.   What do verses 17-18 say about Nehemiah's generosity?_____

_____

_____

_____

_____

The people suffered under the king's tax. By choosing not to use his food allowance, Nehemiah refused to contribute to higher taxes. Instead, his generous table demonstrated that he was willing to share his wealth with others.

Dr. Martin Luther King wrote in one of his sermons, "One of the great tragedies of life is that men seldom bridge the gulf between practice and profession, between doing and saying." Nehemiah bridged that gap. He was a man of his word and a man of action.

MISSION DEBRIEF

Do you do what you say? Do your actions reflect your talk? Are there areas of your life where you need to bridge the gap between what you say and what you do?

Someone is always watching—a spouse, a child, a subordinate, a neighbor. I pray that you and I will always have the courage to walk the talk.

DEEP DIVE

Matthew 5:14-16

"A holy life will produce the deepest impression. Lighthouses blow no horns; they only shine." -D.L. Moody

St. Augustine is the one who coined the term "Sermon on the Mount" for Jesus' teachings in Matthew 5-7. Amidst this compilation is the teaching about being the light of the world. R.T. Kendall explains that this phrase "depicts us [as] both a passive people and an active people. It refers to what we are and what we do."

1. Read Matthew 5:14-15. What does Jesus say about the light?_____

   _____

   _____

   _____

   _____

2. What does Matthew 5:16 encourage us to do, and for what outcome? _____

   _____

   _____

   _____

   _____

MISSION DEBRIEF

3.   How can you be the light where you live, work, and play? _____

_____

_____

_____

_____

What we do matters. It is a reflection of who we are. As Christians, our actions should reflect God and point to him. When we rise up for justice—for what is right—we point others to Jesus. There is power in that truth.

DAY 4

Beware of Smoke Screens

Read Nehemiah 6:1-14

MILITARY FORCES HAVE USED DECEPTION TACTICS SINCE THE dawn of time. *The Art of War*, an ancient military treatise, puts great emphasis on that concept. In the 19ᵗʰ century, a Prussian military analyst, Carl von Clausewitz, pioneered the term "fog of war." That designator captures the uncertainties a person may experience during military operations. "War," he writes, "is the realm of uncertainty; three-quarters of the factors on which action in war is based are wrapped in a fog of greater or lesser uncertainty. A sensitive and discriminating judgment is called for; a skilled intelligence to scent out the truth."

Nehemiah neither read the *Art of War* nor Carl Von Clausewitz's book, but he displayed skilled intelligence and discernment when dealing with his foes. Sanballat and Tobiah had been openly opposed to the building of the wall since the project began. Now that the wall was nearing completion, they switched tactics, directly attacking Nehemiah.

1. Read Nehemiah 6:5-7. What did Sanballat and Tobiah want Nehemiah to believe? _____

_____

_____

_____

MISSION DEBRIEF

2.   What is Nehemiah's response in verses 8-9? What does that say about him? _____

_____

_____

_____

_____

If at first you don't succeed, try, try again. Scaring Nehemiah did not work. But our villains would not quit.

3.   What is Nehemiah encouraged to do in verse 10?_____

_____

_____

_____

_____

4.   Numbers 18 lists the duties of the priesthood. What does Numbers 18:7 say about outsiders

(people who are not priests) entering the temple? _____

_____

_____

_____

_____

5.   What happened to King Uzziah in 2 Chronicles 26:16-20? _____

_____

_____

_____

_____

MISSION DEBRIEF

Their tactics did not fool Nehemiah. He persevered through each attack. His intelligence and discriminating judgment allowed him to discern the truth. Nehemiah also knew better than to confront the opposition.

6. What does Proverbs 26:4 warn about? _____

    _____

    _____

    _____

    _____

7. What promise is expressed in Exodus 14:14? _____

    _____

    _____

    _____

    _____

8. How does Nehemiah's response (Nehemiah 6:14) match those verses? _____

    _____

    _____

    _____

    _____

Discernment is needed when we face unchartered territories. The fog of war can fuel our uncertainties, but God is the strong tower we can always run to (Proverbs 18:10).

Do you need discernment today? Do you seek your way or God's way? Sometimes we feel unjustly handled, when in reality we are acting selfishly. Bring it to God in prayer as you close today's lesson.

MISSION DEBRIEF

DEEP DIVE

Steps to Biblical Discernment

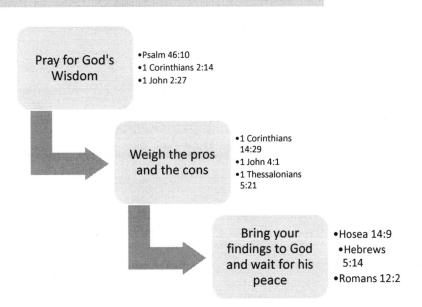

1. In what situations are you needing discernment? _____
   _____
   _____
   _____

2. Use the steps above to decide what to do. _____
   _____
   _____
   _____

I encourage you to look up those verses and choose the one that speaks to you for each step. As you are trying to discern the right thing to do, I also encourage you to pray with a trusted friend and seek her wisdom.

DAY 5

Not a Popularity Contest

Read Nehemiah 5:15-19

AS YOU STUDY YOUR BIBLE, YOU SOON REALIZE THAT FAITH heroes are not always popular:

- Noah suffered ridicule for building an ark.
- Joseph was sold as a slave by his brothers.
- David was mocked by his brothers for being a shepherd.
- Daniel (see last week's Joint Op Intel) was thrown into the lions' den.
- Jesus was crucified.

Fighting for justice God's way is not a popularity contest. Even so, we are tempted to look in the mirror and chant the words of the evil queen, "Mirror, Mirror on the wall, who's the fairest of them all?" Even the disciples struggled with that.

1.   What is the cause of the argument in Luke 22:24? _____

     _____

     _____

     _____

     _____

2.   What is Jesus' answer in Luke 22:25-27? _____

     _____

     _____

     _____

     _____

MISSION DEBRIEF

3.   How can you fight the urge to be popular at all costs? _____

_____

_____

_____

_____

Nehemiah was doing an incredible job in Jerusalem, but he was not seeking to make a name for himself. The work was finished in fifty-two days (Nehemiah 6:15), which was record time. However, Nehemiah was not merely restoring the wall, he was restoring people's lives.

4.   Read Nehemiah 6:16. To whom does he give credit? What does that say about his character?

_____

_____

_____

_____

5.   Who is the popular guy, according to Nehemiah 6:18-19? _____

_____

_____

_____

_____

Lies and flattery blinded the people. Tobiah had them completely fooled. Nehemiah could have chosen to be popular and win the people's vote. He decided instead to stay focused on God and continue to rise up for justice.

MISSION DEBRIEF

6.   What is the promise of Philippians 1:6? _____

_____

_____

_____

_____

Life is a marathon, not a sprint. Like Nehemiah, we can use discernment and choose our path well.

7.   How have you been encouraged by Nehemiah's example? What good habits can you develop to rise up for justice?_____

_____

_____

_____

_____

DEEP DIVE

Psalm 51

Nehemiah is restoring the wall. He is also repairing people's lives and reviving their faith. The topic of revival is coming up in the next chapter—so keep reading.

Sometimes the first step to restoration is confronting the issue or the person. When sin is involved, the right thing is to repent, if you are the one who sinned, or forgive, if you are the one affected by the sin.

Psalm 51 is a beautiful psalm of repentance. David penned it after his affair with Bathsheba. You can read about it in 2 Samuel 11-12.

MISSION DEBRIEF

1. What is the psalmist's lament in verses 1 and 2? _____

    _____

    _____

    _____

    _____

2. Read verses 3, 4, and 5. What does the psalmist confess? _____

    _____

    _____

    _____

    _____

3. According to verses 6, 7, 10, and 12, what does David know God can accomplish? _____

    _____

    _____

    _____

    _____

4. How can you use David's example when dealing with your sins? _____

    _____

    _____

    _____

    _____

Do you need restoration in your life? Start at the cross. Admit your sins, forgive others, and allow God to renew a right spirit within you.

Haggai: God's Messenger

By Kelli Baker

This week, we studied how Nehemiah stood up for what was right in God's eyes. Haggai also stood up for justice. In the book of Haggai, the Babylonian empire had recently collapsed and fell under Persian rule. Darius, king of Persia, issued a decree allowing the return of exiled Israelites to Jerusalem. Over 40,000 Israelites went home.

With their priorities out of order, the Israelites began rebuilding their homes instead of working on rebuilding the temple. God's purpose for their return was to restore the temple of God. When Haggai brought this to their attention, the people declared that it was not time to rebuild the temple. As the messenger of God, Haggai confronted the people.

"Now, therefore, thus says the Lord of hosts: Consider your ways. You have sown much and harvested little. You eat, but you never have enough; you drink, but you never have your fill. You clothe yourselves, but no one is warm. And he who earns wages does so to put them into a bag with holes" (Haggai 1:5-6).

The Lord told Haggai to advise the Israelites of their misplaced priorities. Haggai reminded them that they were foregoing God's blessing, when they chose to please themselves and those around them, rather than God first. While God might continue to provide, he would not bless them abundantly. As Christians, it is imperative that we ask God for discernment in our lives, so that we may walk in his will and receive the blessings he has promised.

"You shall walk in all the way that the Lord your God has commanded you, that you may live, and that it may go well with you, and that you may live long in the land that you shall possess" (Deuteronomy 5:33).

Haggai's purpose – much like we saw with Nehemiah - was to encourage the Israelites to do the right thing. His leadership motivated the people to obey the Lord and complete the rebuilding of the temple. Haggai relentlessly delivered God's message, "I am with you, declares the Lord." (Haggai 1:13b).

The temple was not as beautiful as the one King Solomon built, so the elders were discouraged after only working a month. Again, God used Haggai to encourage the people and remind them of their purpose. The rebuilding was not meant for personal extolment, but for the glorification of the Lord.

"The latter glory of this house shall be greater than the former, says the Lord of hosts. And in this place I will give peace, declares the Lord ..." (Haggai 2:9).

Haggai encouraged the Israelites with the hope of what was to come. Their rebuilding of the temple required courage, but God promised to be with them. In the same manner, he will be with us as we obey his call in our lives.

It may require us to have courage to stand up for our convictions and go against the grain, instead of following the crowd. But that's okay. God promises to be with us. We may even find that our courage allows others to step out and stand up for what's right as well.

Peace-Making

Habits to Outcome

By Melissa Hicks

> *Blessed are the peacemakers, for they shall be called sons of God. - Matthew 5:9*

Nehemiah chapter five offers a unique perspective on peace-making. Nehemiah addresses the injustices the Jews experienced in a seemingly confrontational and condemning way. However, rather than fighting solely for justice's sake, Nehemiah targets the heart of the people. In calling for repentance, he restores peace and unity to the community.

As believers, we are also called to make peace. At times, our approach might mirror Nehemiah's methods. Or perhaps our peacemaking will resemble Jesus' exhortation to "turn the other cheek" (Matthew 5:39). Whatever method the Lord calls us to use, reconciliation and restoration are the goal.

ACTIONS TO PREVENT CONFLICT:

- Be kind to others, tenderhearted, forgiving one another as Christ forgave you (Ephesians 4:32).
- Speak the truth (Ephesians 4:25).
- Assume good will (1 Corinthians 13:4-7).

GUIDELINES FOR CONFLICT RESOLUTION:

- Ask God for discernment (James 1:5).
- Search your heart (Matthew 7:3-5).
- Pray for the other person/party involved (Matthew 5:44).
- Confront personally and quickly, in love, always with the goal of restoration (Matthew 18:15-17).
- Absorb the injustice. Take the higher road rather than seek vengeance (Matthew 5:39-45). This can be a powerful tool to point people to Christ, but discernment is a must.
- No matter what happens, practice forgiveness (1 Peter 4:8).
- "If possible, so far as it depends on you, live peaceably with all" (Romans 12:18)

Week 4
Rise Up for a Revival

The most glorious moments in your life are not the so-called days of success, but rather those days when out of dejection and despair you feel rise in you a challenge to life, and the promise of future accomplishments.

- GUSTAVE FLAUBERT

27 April 1994 – Pretoria, South Africa

IN THE MIDST OF INTERNAL VIOLENCE, AN ELECTION WAS TAKING place that would forever change the political landscape of South Africa. Nelson Mandela, who had been a political prisoner for 27 years, became the first elected black president.

"Presiding over the transition from apartheid minority rule to a multicultural democracy, Mandela saw national reconciliation as the primary task of his presidency."

Emphasizing personal forgiveness and reconciliation, he sought to restore a country destroyed by hatred and distrust. Often criticized by both his peers and his enemies, Nelson Mandela never wavered from his ultimate goal: heal the past and foster a better future. Controversial at times, he stayed true to his devotion to democracy, equality, and learning.

At a fundraising event in 2008, he exhorted the younger generation to continue the good fight – "It is in your hands to make of our world a better one for all."

Apartheid ended 30 years ago. There is still a lot to rebuild; but one man laid the first stone in the wall against Apartheid. Nelson Mandela rose up for a revival in his country.

This week we will study the importance of revival, and why we need it in our lives.

Sustainment Operations

A common term in the military is sustainment operation. It can be defined as "the provision of personnel, logistics, and other support required to maintain and prolong operations or combat until successful accomplishment or revision of the mission or of the national objective."

The wall was finished; but Nehemiah was well aware that his job was not over. He needed to protect what had been built. For starters, Jerusalem needed to be populated again, and God's people needed a spiritual revival. It was time for sustainment operations.

It is Not about Me

When we are in charge of a project, it is tempting to try to do it all on our own. I have often struggled with the belief that I should have all the qualifications and all the answers. The reality is, God will surround me with people to help and support me. A wall is built brick by brick. When I overlook my shortcomings and soldier on with the task, I am left with holes in my project. I need others to fill in the gap. That's why everybody has a place at the wall.

Nehemiah was aware of his strengths *and* his limitations. As an insightful leader, he enlisted the help of qualified people - the most important attributes being God-fearing and faithful (Nehemiah 7:2). Nehemiah appointed them, but he also built them up. When he gave Ezra center stage in Chapter 8, he built him a platform, so that the message could be heard by all.

Revival of the Soul

"Fair is foul and foul is fair," claim the three witches of Macbeth. A compelling tale of greed, power, and jealousy, Macbeth demonstrates that appearances can be deceiving. When God asked Samuel to anoint Israel's next king, he warned him about appearances, "For the Lord sees not as man sees: man looks on the outward appearance, but the Lord looks on the heart" (1 Samuel 16:7). King David came to be known as "a man after God's own heart" (Acts 13:22).

All our works and efforts are pointless when our hearts and minds are far from God. To properly rebuild, Nehemiah knew that God's people needed a revival of the soul. The wall might give the appearance of strength, but if the hearts of the people are far from God, the wall will not stand.

Are you ready to seek God and be renewed by him? Me too. Let's see what God has for us this week.

WEEK 4

MISSION DEBRIEF

DAY 1

DAY 2

DAY 3

DAY 4

DAY 5

JOINT OP INTEL

H2O

Revival is in the Air

Read Nehemiah 7:1-4

UNFAZED BY CONTINUED ATTACKS AND OPPOSITION, NEHEMIAH continued his rebuilding efforts by appointing officers and assistants in key positions. The people we surround ourselves with have a tremendous influence on our lives. Choosing them wisely is essential.

1.   What qualities does Exodus 18:21 invite us to seek in people we serve/work with?_____

_____

_____

_____

_____

2.   How did Nehemiah describe Hananiah in chapter 7, verse 2?_____

_____

_____

_____

Throughout history, defensive walls have been necessary to survive in an ever-changing world of invasion and conquest. Building a wall is an acceptable start, but guarding the wall is crucial.

MISSION DEBRIEF

3. What was Nehemiah doing in Nehemiah 7:3? What was he anticipating? _____

_____

_____

_____

_____

Nehemiah did not wait for an attack. He readied himself for it. Faith, not fear, was his motivator. We have in Jesus a strong foundation. Whom shall we fear? When all is well, it is tempting to let our guard down. In combat, it is a matter of life and death. As believers, we need to be alert and watchful at all times.

4. What did Jesus expect of his disciples in Luke 21:36? _____

_____

_____

_____

_____

5. Why should we follow that advice according to Ephesians 5:16? _____

_____

_____

_____

_____

6. What is Peter's exhortation in 1 Peter 5:8-9? _____

_____

_____

_____

_____

MISSION DEBRIEF

7.   How can you be watchful? What practical steps can you take? _____

_____

_____

_____

_____

We need to be vigilant, lest we fall prey to our sworn enemy, the devil. Don't wait for the attack — anticipate and be ready.

DEEP DIVE

Readiness

Innovative Readiness Training (IRT) is a Department of Defense (DoD) military training opportunity. The joint training opportunities increase deployment readiness. Nehemiah practiced readiness. He anticipated potential attacks and ensured he was ready.

Do you ever face harsh times? Do you have people in your life who are difficult to handle? Do you consider life to be tough? (Do you like rhetorical questions?)

1.   What does 1 Peter 4:12 say about trials in our lives? _____

_____

_____

_____

_____

MISSION DEBRIEF

2. What practical steps is he giving in 1 Peter 5:6-10?_____

_____

_____

_____

_____

3. What steps/disciplines will you practice this week? _____

_____

_____

_____

_____

Why should we practice spiritual readiness? A.W. Tozer explained it this way in his devotional, *Renewed Day by Day.*

The evangelical church has come through a period when nearly everyone has believed that there is just one prerequisite to readiness—being born again. We have made being born again almost like receiving a pass to a special event; when Jesus returns, we whip out the pass to prove our readiness. Frankly, I do not think it will be like that. I do not believe that all professed believers are automatically ready to meet the Lord. Our Savior Himself was joined by Peter, John, and Paul in warning and pleading that we should live, watch, and pray so to be ready for Jesus' coming.

How can we practice spiritual readiness? It is a discipline, and like all disciplines, it requires commitment and perseverance. The outcome far outweighs the cost. Are you in?

DAY 2

We Will Rise

Read Nehemiah 7:5-73

WARNING: *LONG LIST OF NAMES AHEAD. STICK WITH ME. THEY have a purpose, and we'll make it through this together.*

We discussed in Week 2 the concept of identity in light of spiritual warfare. God has more to say on this topic.

Established on January 1, 1892, Ellis Island became the busiest immigrant inspection station. Today, many Americans can go to the Ellis Island website and search for information about their ancestors. Do you know your ancestry? Does your lineage take you back to Europe, Africa, or maybe Asia? Most of us long to know who our ancestors were, where they came from, and what they did. It is part of our identity.

> **IDENTITY**
>
> condition or character as to who a person or what a thing is; the qualities, beliefs, etc., that distinguish or identify a person or thing.

In order to establish proper lineage, Nehemiah located a document of all the exiles.

1. Read Nehemiah 7:6-7.

    a. Who are the people listed?_____

    _____

    b. Who came with them? _____

    _____

    c. Why do you suppose this was significant to Nehemiah? _____

    _____

MISSION DEBRIEF

Nehemiah's purpose was to repopulate Jerusalem (see verse 4). Jerusalem was more than just a city. It was where God's temple was located and where his presence dwelt. It was the city of God's people and a crucial part of their identity. It needed to be populated by the right men and women.

Those lists of names in Nehemiah represent more than just people. They speak of God's unending love and redemptive power. The people had strayed and disobeyed God. Judgment was upon them (see Jeremiah 20:4), but God prepared a way for them to come back to him.

2.   Read Ezekiel 11:14-20. What is the promise? _____

_____

_____

_____

_____

"The important thing is not to count the people but to realize that these people counted." The most beautiful thing about those genealogies is that they lead to Jesus (Matthew 1; Luke 1). God redeemed them so that you and I could one day be redeemed too.

3.   What does John 1:12-13 say about those of us who are believers?_____

_____

_____

_____

_____

4.   How does this truth affect you today?_____

_____

_____

_____

_____

MISSION DEBRIEF

Girlfriends, do not skip over this. This is us. We are children of God. Finish today with a prayer of thanksgiving.

Maybe you are reading this and have not yet accepted Jesus as your Lord and Savior. Only by doing so can you be part of his family. Would you pause and pray about it? If you have questions, check out the Planting Roots website (plan of salvation) or talk with a trusted Christian friend.

DEEP DIVE

Identity

On 9/11, terrorists attacked landmarks that were symbols of the American identity. The towers represented our financial power, and the Pentagon our military power. The suspected third target was the White House, which represents our political power. Attacking those meant attacking our identity.

Fake ID and identity theft are not solely 21st-century topics. They are also spiritual issues that are as old as time. If your identity is not firmly rooted in God, you are easy prey for the devil's schemes (Ephesians 6:11).

Here are some truths God speaks over you (You can go back to Week 2, Day 2 for more verses):

- You are His beloved (Jeremiah 31: 3).
- You are His child (1 John 3:1).
- He delights in you (Zephaniah 3:17).
- You are forgiven (1 Peter 2:24).
- You are a co-heir with Christ (Romans 8:17).
- You are set apart (1 Peter 2:9).
- You are wonderfully made (Psalm 139:14).
- You are a masterpiece (Ephesians 2:10).

Which truth do you need the most today? I encourage you to write the verse on a notecard or a sticky note and use it as a reminder.

We Cry Holy

Read Nehemiah 8:1-8

*B*UT WHEN THE SEVENTH MONTH HAD *come, the people of Israel were in their towns. Nehemiah 7:73b.*

The seventh month is significant in the Jewish faith. They refer to it as the month of Teshuva, meaning repentance. On the first of the month is Rosh Hashanah – the Jewish New Year. Yom Kippur follows ten days later – the holiest day of the Jewish calendar.

Their hearts and minds were ready to receive the Word of God.

The Bible is not a book of spells that can change our lives simply because we read it. We need to understand it.

> In Rabbinical Judaism, *Rosh Hashanah* (literally "the head of the year") is celebrated as Jewish New Year's Day. The holiday is observed on the first two days of the Hebrew month of Tishri, which usually falls in September or October, and marks the beginning of a ten-day period of prayer, self-examination, and repentance, which culminates on the fasting day of Yom Kippur.

1. What benefits from meditating on God's Word does Psalm 1:3-4 list? _____

_____

_____

_____

_____

Ezra (check this week's Joint Op Intel) is entering the stage. He will be the key player for the next two chapters.

2.

MISSION DEBRIEF

3.   Read Nehemiah 8:1-8.

   a.   What does Ezra bring with him? _____

   _____

   b.   What are his helpers doing? _____

   _____

   c.   Why is it essential for the people to understand the Word of God? _____

   _____

   _____

   d.   What can you do if you do not understand what you read in the Bible? _____

   _____

   _____

   The Torah (the first five books of the Bible – what Ezra brought with him) is the foundation of the Jewish religion and civil law. Is the Bible the foundation for your life?

4.   There are many benefits to obeying God's commands. Which ones are listed in Psalm

   119:9-11? _____

   _____

   _____

   _____

   _____

A life devoted to studying God's Word is a life built on a strong foundation (Matthew 6:24-27). Do you need a revival? It begins with God. Do you need a renewed heart? It starts with reading his Word and applying it to our lives (see H2O).

MISSION DEBRIEF

DEEP DIVE

Parable of the Sower

Intro para

1. Read Matthew 13:1-9,18-23 and fill out this chart. The first one is done for you.

Verse	Soil	Effect on the seed	Verse	Explanation
3	*Path*	*Eaten by birds*	18	*Word of God was not understood*
5-6			20-21	
7			22	
8			23	

2. What can you do to make sure you have good soil so that the Word of God can take root in your life? If you need ideas and suggestions, look up this week's H2O. _____

_____

_____

_____

_____

DAY 4

Reign Above It All

Read Nehemiah 8:9-12

HEBREWS 4:12 TELLS US THAT THE WORD OF GOD IS SHARPER than any two-edged sword. Have you ever experienced conviction and grief from something you read in the Bible? The Israelites found themselves in a unique situation as they faced the reality of their transgressions for the first time. Some of them had not understood or even heard the teachings of the Torah.

1. What was the people's reaction in Nehemiah 8:9?_____

_____

_____

_____

_____

2. Mourning was the natural reaction after they were convicted of their sins. What were the

    exhortations from Nehemiah, Ezra, and the Levites? _____

_____

_____

_____

_____

Their sins were many, but God's grace is greater. Conviction led to confession and repentance. What was their attitude at the end of the day according to Nehemiah 8:12?

The joy of the Lord is your strength. This beautiful truth can be a reality in our lives as well.

MISSION DEBRIEF

The Bible has a lot to say about joy. It is a concept closely related to faith.

3. Match these verses to what they say about joy:

Psalm 4:7	Rejoice in the God of my salvation
Psalm 30:5	Fruit of the spirit
Habakkuk 3:18	More joy than grain and wine
John 15:11	Joy comes in the morning
Galatians 5:22	Your joy may be full

Joy comes from God. The secret to joy is to believe what God says and act upon it. His mercy and forgiveness will always allow us to come back to him and be restored. Joy that is not based on faith is fleeting at best. Faith-based joy is the fuel we need to weather the storms of life.

4. What promises of God bring you joy today? _____

_____

_____

_____

_____

YOM KIPPUR

Yom Kippur means "Day of Atonement." It is the holiest day of the year for Jews. For nearly 26 hours they "afflict their souls" by abstaining from food and drink, not washing or applying lotions or creams, not wearing leather footwear, and abstaining from marital relations. Instead, they spend the day in the synagogue, praying for forgiveness.

Leviticus 16:30;
Leviticus 23:23-32

MISSION DEBRIEF

DEEP DIVE

Fruit of the Spirit

What is a revival? It can be many things. But the word is most often used to describe a situation where many people seek God wholeheartedly, strive for obedience, confess their sins, and experience the joy and freedom of walking with God. It starts with earnest prayer.

1. What is the psalmist's cry in Psalm 85:4? Can you paraphrase it and make it your prayer? Our hearts and minds are the epic centers for a genuine revival. Our hearts need to be turned to God, and our minds focused on the Spirit. God will restore us. What is an evidence of revival? We will display more of the fruit of the Spirit. _____

    _____

    _____

    _____

    _____

2. Read Galatians 5:19-23 and fill out the chart below.

Verse	Fruit of the flesh	Verse	Fruit of the Spirit
19		22	
20		23	
21			

3. Look at the chart and identify your fruit. _____

    _____

    _____

    _____

    _____

MISSION DEBRIEF

4. Is the root of your fruit Christ or something else? Do you need a revival? What can you do about it? _____

_____

_____

_____

_____

Finish today by giving thanks and asking God for strength to walk in the Spirit. Let your fruit reflect where your heart is.

DAY 5

Send Me

Read Nehemiah 8:13-18

THE FEAST OF BOOTHS OR TABERNACLES IS A TIME OF celebration. It follows Rosh Hashanah and Yom Kippur. For seven days, the Israelites rejoiced about their renewed relationship with God. They lived in tents to display their dependence upon God's care and provision. It is the most joyful of Jewish feasts. This was especially true of the feast mentioned in Nehemiah.

> Sukkot (Feast of Booths) is observed in the fall, from the 15th to the 22nd of Tishri. During this time many Jewish families construct a *sukkah* - a small hastily built hut in which meals are eaten throughout the festival.
>
> The sukkah reminds people of the tents Israel lived in during their 40-year journey in the wilderness after the exodus from Egypt.
>
> Leviticus 23:33-44
> Leviticus 23:33-44

1. What was the atmosphere according to Nehemiah 8:17? _____

_____

_____

_____

_____

The joy experienced that week was comparable to the joy experienced by the Israelites under Joshua, when they finally entered the Promised Land. In this chapter, Ezra set the stage for a new culture. He not only brought the Word of God to them, but he took the time to explain it so that the people understood. This led to a revival of their faith and a renewal in their hearts. It only takes a spark to light a fire. Ezra and Nehemiah were that spark.

2. Read the following verses and record what they are encouraging you to do.

    a.   Romans 12:11-12 _____

         _____

    b.   Matthew 5:16 _____

         _____

    c.   James 5:16_____

         _____

    d.   Isaiah 6:8_____

         _____

3. Can God begin a revival with you? Can you be the spark? If so, where and when? Maybe the culture you are in is toxic (coarse language, inappropriate behaviors, etc.). You could wait for someone to set a different tone, or you can rise up and let change begin with you. _____

_____

_____

_____

_____

MISSION DEBRIEF

DEEP DIVE

Psalm 27

Psalm 27 is traditionally read during the Feast of Tabernacles. It is a beautiful way for us to end our study this week.

1. Read Psalm 27 slowly and reflect on the following questions:

    a. What are you afraid of (verse 1)? _____

    _____

    b. Why should you not be afraid (verse 5)? _____

    _____

    c. Military members don't learn to do battle in the classroom. They learn *about* doing battle in the classroom. Where should we learn about life according to verse 11?_____

    _____

    d. The ultimate joy is not God's gifts but God himself. What is the psalmist's plea in verse 4? _____

    _____

2. What practical steps can you take today to make verses 13 and 14 a reality in your life?_____

    _____

    _____

    _____

    _____

JOINT OP INTEL

Ezra: Associate of Nehemiah

By Kelli Baker

Unlike the past three Joint Op Intel leaders we learned about, Ezra worked alongside Nehemiah in the rebuilding of the people. Last week, we learned that Haggai's message was to encourage the people to continue rebuilding the temple in Jerusalem. With this accomplished, the people needed help getting back to God's Word. In those times, the luxury of owning a Torah was reserved for the priests and teachers of the Law. Help was needed to carry the scrolls of the Word as they taught.

God gave Ezra, his obedient servant, favor in the eyes of the king. The King chose Ezra and gave him the authority to appoint judges and magistrates in Jerusalem to uphold the law of the Lord, stating that, "all such as know the laws of your God. And those who do not know, you shall teach them" (Ezra 7:25). Once Ezra taught the Israelites the Law of the Lord, the judges and magistrates would uphold God's law.

Prior to his arrival in Jerusalem, Ezra worked as a scribe in Babylon. (Scribes were to copy royal and sacred manuscripts.) Not only did Ezra write the manuscripts, he spent time pondering them. God chose Ezra to bring the Word back to his people because Ezra dedicated his life to studying God's Word.

"For Ezra had set his heart to study of Law of the Lord, and to do it and to teach his statues and rules in Israel" (Ezra 7:10).

A learned man, dedicated to teaching the Law, Ezra carefully spoke of the courage that it took to tackle this task.

"I took courage, for the hand of the Lord my God was on me, and I gathered leading men from Israel to go up with me" (Ezra 7:27.)

We have been learning that it requires great courage to rise up and lead as God calls us. We may even feel unqualified for the position. However, when we step out in faith and courage, we realize that God fills the gap. Where we are weak, he is strong. Jesus says to Paul in 2 Corinthians 12:9a, "My grace is sufficient for you, for my power is made perfect in weakness." Ezra demonstrates how to allow the power of God to be made perfect in what may feel is weakness.

We also learned in our study this week about how Ezra used God's Word to reveal God's truth to the Israelites. They began to understand that they were living in sin. "He who has ears to hear, let him hear" (Matthew 11:15) is Jesus' plea to us. God's Word will actively reveal sins in our lives too.

Knowing God's Word and putting it into practice are two different things. Prior to Ezra's arrival, the Israelites were unaware of their transgressions. They had been living far from their culture, and much of God's Word had not been passed down through the generations.

Ezra knew his purpose was to restore the Word of God to the people through repentance, and he was prepared to direct the people as their eyes began to open. Along with Nehemiah and the Levites, Ezra encouraged the people to stop weeping and celebrate because of the deliverance the Lord had given to them.

Ezra was sent to teach and uphold the law of the Lord that had been erased due to the years spent in bondage. They had forgotten their true identity while living in exile. Listening to Ezra's faithful teaching, the people repented and were restored.

Fortunately, we have the opportunity to come to repentance through Christ. We are blessed to have the ability to read God's Word anytime and anywhere, unlike the Israelites during Ezra's time.

God has paved a new way to connect with him through the ultimate sacrifice of Jesus Christ. Understanding that our identity is found in Christ is paramount to repentance and restoration.

"For he himself is our peace, who has made us both one and has broken down in his flesh the dividing wall of hostility by abolishing the law of commandments expressed in ordinances, that he might create in himself one new man in place of the two" (Ephesians 2:14-15).

Studying the Bible with Others

Habits to Outcome

By Melissa Hicks

> They read from the book, from the Law of God, clearly, and they gave the sense, so that the people understood the reading...On the second day the heads of fathers' houses of all the people, with priests and the Levites, came together to Ezra the scribe in order to study the words of the Law. (Nehemiah 8:8, 13)

Have you ever opened the Bible, started reading, and then wondered, "What in the world did that mean?" No matter how long we've walked with Jesus, there are still parts of the Bible that are difficult to understand. However, that doesn't mean we should give up and skip over those parts. God wants us to love him with our hearts and our *minds* (Matthew 22:34-40). We need to engage with the Bible, not only with feelings and sentiments, but with brainpower and intellect. The best way to do this is to join a group of people (a church, a Bible study, a mentor) who can study the Bible with you.

BENEFITS:

- Protects the truth: helping us to observe what the Bible says, what it means, and what we should do about it (https://www.desiringgod.org/articles/read-the-bible-with-someone-else).

- Discipleship: commitment to each other's spiritual growth (https://www.desiringgod.org/interviews/what-is-discipleship-and-how-is-it-done).

- Accountability: assistance in staying faithful to God's ways https://www.desiringgod.org/articles/why-accountability-matters).

MISSION DEBRIEF

TIPS FOR STUDYING WITH OTHERS:

- Pray.
- Read the passage several times throughout the week.
- Read before and after the passage to get the context.
- Take notes:
- Who? What? Where? When? Why?
- What's the main idea?
- What do I not understand?
- What do I learn about God, others, or myself?
- What does this confirm or change in me theologically/practically?
- What do I need to do (through the Holy Spirit's power) as a result of this passage?
- Read a commentary (The ESV Study Bible provides excellent insight).
- Discuss the passage with others in your group.
- Ask questions.
- Emphasize application, not just knowledge.

WEEK 5
RISE UP AND REMEMBER

Those who do not remember the past are condemned to relive it.

—GEORGE SANTAYANA

November 19, 1863 – Gettysburg

"**F**OUR SCORE AND SEVEN YEARS AGO." THIS ICONIC PHRASE begins the 271 words President Lincoln delivered at the dedication of the Soldiers' National Cemetery in Gettysburg, Pennsylvania. Only four and a half months after the Union defeated the Confederacy at Gettysburg, Lincoln reminded the audience that the Civil War represented a test that would determine whether the nation could endure.

Four years of intense combat left between 620,000 and 750,000 dead. A nation would need to heal from deep wounds, and a significant divide emerged between the north and the south. The country, especially the south, had been utterly destroyed. It would be a long road to rebuilding. Gettysburg was a place to reflect and remember. Lincoln eloquently expressed that feeling, "The world will little note, nor long remember what we say here, but it can never forget what they did here. It is for us the living, rather, to be dedicated here to the unfinished work which they who fought here have thus far so nobly advanced."

President Lincoln encouraged the nation to rise up from the ashes and remember.

The Road to War

History has its share of conflicts and wars. None has been as bloody, terrifying, and impactful as World War I. Trench warfare and mustard gas were the backdrops for one of the largest wars in history. I remember driving through Verdun, France as a child and seeing fields still empty of vegetation and trees. I also remember graves with the simple inscription, "A Soldier of the Great War, Known to

God." It was supposed to be the war to end all wars. Yet twenty-one years later marked the beginning of World War II.

The road to war is a concept that emerged after WWII. How did we get there? What did we miss? Could this have been avoided? Unless we face history and face ourselves, we will repeat our mistakes. As Aldous Huxley cleverly wrote, "That men do not learn much from the lessons of history is the most important of all the lessons that history has to teach."

The People of Israel Confess Their Sin

Mourning and fasting, the Israelites gather around Ezra. After hearing the words of the Torah, they all rise up and listen to Ezra's prayer, a prayer of remembrance and repentance. Our past can hold us back and bring us down, but we need to deal with it. In the hands of a loving and merciful God, our past failures and sorrows can be redeemed.

Let's go down memory lane!

WEEK 5

MISSION DEBRIEF

DAY 1

DAY 2

DAY 3

DAY 4

DAY 5

JOINT OP INTEL

H2O

DAY 1

What Would You Do?

Read Nehemiah 9:1-5

THE FEAST OF TABERNACLES HAS ENDED, AND THE FEASTING turned to fasting as the Word of God convicted the people of their sins. Their fast led them to confession and eventually to worship. Chapter nine in Nehemiah captured this fantastic process. I love this progression. It speaks of God's promise, "weeping may tarry for the night, but joy comes with the morning." (Psalm 30:5). We can learn from them and follow their pattern.

1. Read Nehemiah 9:2-3. How are the Israelites dealing with their sins?_____

_____

_____

_____

_____

They did not merely confront their sins but also the sins of their fathers. Dealing with your past is critical. We will go more into that on Day 3.

It can be overwhelming to be convicted of a specific sin and stop there. It can lead to guilt and shame. Have you ever felt shame? I have. The good news is, God does not want us to live in shame.

2. What does Romans 10:11 say about shame?_____

_____

_____

_____

_____

MISSION DEBRIEF

If we believe in Jesus and have confessed our sins, we will not be put to shame. Our sins have been nailed to the cross. This should spark worship.

Let's go back to Nehemiah.

3.   According to Nehemiah 9:3, what prompted their confession? _____

_____

_____

_____

_____

4.   What does Hebrews 4:12 say about God's Word? _____

_____

_____

_____

_____

The prompt for our conviction and spiritual grief can be from a friend, a sermon, or something we read in a book. But we always need to go back to the Bible. It speaks the truth about our sins and shows us what needs to change.

5.   Read John 8:31-32. What power is there in the truth of God? _____

_____

_____

_____

_____

Who does not want freedom? I cannot speak for you, but I want freedom from guilt and shame. I want freedom from carrying a secret too long. Do you? Unburden yourself and confess. This model of confession is an excellent way to turn your sorrows into joy.

MISSION DEBRIEF

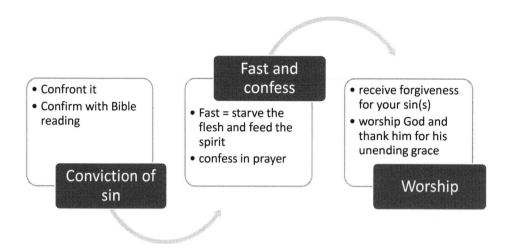

Are you convicted of a particular sin? Do not hold on to your guilt and shame. Confess it to a loving God and watch your tears turn into songs of praise.

DEEP DIVE

Isaiah 58

Fasting is a spiritual discipline seldom practiced. I have found in my personal experience that prayer and fasting are a powerful duo.

WORD FOR YOKE IN MATTHEW 6	WORD FOR YOKE IN ISAIAH 58
ζυγός zygos	מוֹטָה mô·ṭā(h)
yoke; balance scale	yoke bar; oppression; carrying-pole

What is fasting? It can be defined as abstaining from something, usually food, for religious commitment or as an expression of repentance. My definition is "starving the flesh and feeding the spirit." You may choose to abstain from food, television, social media, shopping, and more, and replace it with prayer, Bible reading or studying, meditating on scripture, and such.

MISSION DEBRIEF

Isaiah 58 gives us a clear picture of the fast God is looking for. This might help you discern how to organize your fast.

1. Read Isaiah 58:5-7 and list the attitudes God is looking for. What character trait is highlighted in verse 5? Is it true or false humility? _____

    _____

    _____

    _____

    _____

2. Read Matthew 6:16-18. What does it say about false humility, and how can we guard ourselves from it? _____

    _____

    _____

    _____

    _____

3. Why should we humble ourselves, as stated in 1 Peter 5:6-7? _____

    _____

    _____

    _____

    _____

MISSION DEBRIEF

4. According to the passage in Isaiah, a fast will break every yoke. A yoke here represents a burden, a bondage. It is a metaphor that talks about the things that tie us to worldly things. Read Matthew 11:29. Whose yoke are we supposed to carry? Why? _____

_____

_____

_____

_____

5. Read Isaiah 58:8-9. What promises are listed there? _____

_____

_____

_____

_____

Sincere fasting will allow us to be closer to God by humbling ourselves and doing the things that matter most (verses 6-7). Our sins can weigh us down. Consider fasting as a powerful companion to your confession time.

DAY 2

The Heart of The Matter

Read Nehemiah 9:6-15

HAVE YOU EVER OBSERVED HOW SIMPLY CHANGING YOUR position gives you a different perspective? A city will look different from the sky than on the ground. A lighthouse will appear smaller from a distance. Having the correct angle can change everything.

You may or may not have experienced the joy and panic of last-minute PCS orders. Maybe you think you still have another year at your current duty station; but instead, you are moving in a month. Or when the orders come, you discover you are not moving to the east coast, but overseas. If I expect the DOD (Department of Defense) to send me where they promised and when they promised, I will be disappointed. Unmet expectations are sometimes the consequence of a weak outlook.

That same concept applies to our spiritual life. We need to remind ourselves who God is and where he is. We need to align ourselves with his point of view.

1. What is Ecclesiastes 5:2 reminding us? _____
    _____
    _____
    _____

2. What additional intel does Isaiah 55:8-9 give us on that concept? _____
    _____
    _____
    _____

The Israelites started their confession time by recognizing God's power and majesty.

MISSION DEBRIEF

3.   Read Nehemiah 9:6-15 and fill out the chart below.

Verse	What it says about God
6	*Maker of heaven and earth*
8	
9-10	
11	
12	
13	
14	
15	

My perspective on life changes dramatically when I remember God's place and power. When I know who is in control, I no longer have to worry about the situation I'm in.

4.   What beautiful promise can be found in Colossians 1:17? _____

_____

_____

_____

5.   How does this truth change your perspective on any situation you may be facing today? _____

_____

_____

_____

I encourage you to spend the rest of today meditating on that truth. Let it sink in and bring you peace.

MISSION DEBRIEF

DEEP DIVE

Selah

If you've spent any time in the Psalms, you may have come across the term Selah. Its actual meaning is unclear, but most commentaries believe it is a musical instruction calling for a break. Do you need a break? More often than not, we need to hit the pause button in our fast-paced world.

1. Psalm 46:10 is a beautiful verse that might be known to you. Here are a few different translations. Which one speaks to you today? Why should you pause? _____

_____

_____

_____

ESV	Be still, and know that I am God. I will be exalted among the nations, I will be exalted in the earth!
NASB	Cease striving and know that I am God; I will be exalted among the nations, I will be exalted in the earth.
HCSB	Stop your fighting—and know that I am God, exalted among the nations, exalted on the earth.
The Message	Step out of the traffic! Take a long, loving look at me, your High God, above politics, above everything.

Being still is tough when your to-do list is never-ending, and you are under the pressures of time and people. Yet being still is not a waste of time. It is a time to refuel. It will invigorate you and fill you with God's peace and presence.

DAY 3

Turning Graveyards into Gardens

Read Nehemiah 9:16-37.

WHO WE ARE IS DIRECTLY SHAPED BY OUR ROOTS. PUT ANOTHER way, our *past* has shaped our *present*. Whether we admit to it or not, our family of origin (going back three of four generations) has molded us into who we are today. Even our language recognizes that truth. Finish the following sentences for me:

- Like mother like _____.
- The apple does not fall far from _____.

Today's reading takes us down memory lane, as we consider all the mistakes and sins the Israelites committed over hundreds of years. Why are they doing that? It's not fun to remember a shady past or admit that our family is a bit dysfunctional. Is it necessary? Is it wise? Here's the truth: God wants us to remember and deal with our past. He has good reasons.

Allow me to further that point by turning to science. Rachel Yehuda, a researcher in the field of epigenetics, conducted a study on mass trauma victims and their offspring. "Their latest results reveal descendants of people who survived the Holocaust have different stress hormone profiles than their peers, perhaps predisposing them to anxiety disorders."

Further results have shown parents or grandparents who were underfed before puberty would have offspring more likely dealing with diabetes and heart disease. It is crazy to think that traumatic experiences can modify our DNA.

Most of us are familiar with statistics regarding children of alcoholics or physically abusive parents. A dangerous pattern is created and often repeated. Whether we think it is fair or not, our past and the sins of our ancestors shape us. Not every family is dysfunctional, but no one is perfect.

The good news—it does not need to stay that way. The power to make a change lies within us through the gift of the Holy Spirit (Philippians 4:13). We can choose to rise up and remember in

MISSION DEBRIEF

order to heal and move forward. Let's go back to Nehemiah and observe how the Israelites dealt with their shady past.

1.   Read Nehemiah 9:35. Are the people who lived in the days of Nehemiah responsible for the

     sins mentioned? _____

     _____

     _____

     _____

     _____

2.   Yet here they are confessing those sins. Read Nehemiah 9:32-33 and try to determine why

     they are exposing family secrets and confessing of their own wickedness at the same time.

     From their knowledge of God's character, they knew that healing and forgiveness were available to them. God is just and merciful. Iniquities do not go unpunished, but his mercy and grace always prevail.

3.   Read Exodus 34:6-7.

     a.   According to that passage, to how many generations does God keep his steadfast love? _

          _____

     b.   To how many generations will he punish their sins?_____

          _____

     c.   Circle where you see the scale tipping.

                    mercy   judgment

Acknowledging the sins of our family of origin can be painful. For some it will require professional help. But God gives us the power to end unhealthy behaviors and create a better future for our children. The benefits are steadfast love and faithfulness. Do you want that? I certainly do.

MISSION DEBRIEF

Today's study can bring forth many emotions. I encourage you to share them with a trusted friend. Pray with her, and seek professional help, if needed.

DEEP DIVE

Father Abraham

Abraham is one of the well-known patriarchs of the Old Testament. You can read his beautiful story of faith and obedience in the Book of Genesis. Ordered by God to leave his home and travel to a promised land, Abraham was faithful to the call. He, his wife Sarah, and their household traveled from Ur to Canaan. He was not perfect, however (none of us are). A sin he committed became a generational sin. Here is the family tree:

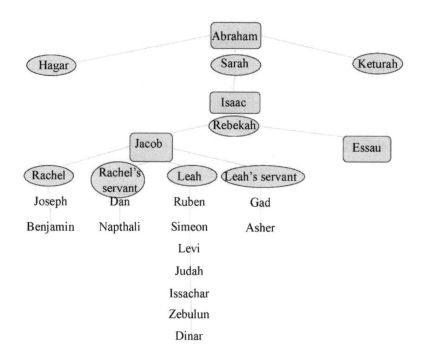

Let's fill out this chart to see what happened.

MISSION DEBRIEF

Verse	Protagonist	Observed behavior
Genesis 12:10-13		
Genesis 20:1-2		
Genesis 26:6-7		
Genesis 27:18-19		
Genesis 37:26-33		

Lies, misogyny, favoritism, sibling rivalry—all those deeply ingrained family sins are displayed in Abraham's descendants. God can and will forgive when we recognize and confess the sin. The pattern can be broken, and our history can be redeemed.

1.   Read Philippians 1:6. What promise do we have that these patterns can be broken? _____

_____

_____

_____

_____

Could God Be This Good?

Read Nehemiah 9:16-37

TODAY, WE WILL BE COVERING THE SAME PASSAGE, BUT WITH A different focus: God's provision. God provides because of who he is, not because of what we do.

During their prayer of remembrance, the Israelites highlighted the times God showed up for them.

1. Look up the verses below and list God's provision

Verse	Provision
Nehemiah 9:11	
Nehemiah 9:15	
Nehemiah 9:20	
Nehemiah 9:22	

God took care of them, as they wandered through the wilderness and entered the Promised Land. He also took care of them while they were in captivity. Those concepts are not merely Old Testament truths. They still apply today.

2. Read John 6:35. Who does Jesus say he is? How can you apply that to your life? _____

_____

_____

_____

_____

3. John 8:12 records another critical statement from Jesus. How is this truth important for you today?_____

_____

_____

_____

_____

It gives me great peace knowing that God provides. The other thing I tend to struggle with (and maybe you do too) is worrying about the future. I have found that when I worry, I mistakenly feel that God does not provide enough.

4. How can Jesus' words in Matthew 6:34 help with this issue? _____

_____

_____

_____

_____

Psalm 104:14-15 draws a beautiful picture of God setting the table for us, "You cause the grass to grow for the livestock and plants for man to cultivate, that he may bring forth food from the earth and wine to gladden the heart of man, oil to make his face shine and bread to strengthen man's heart." God is setting a table for you and me with all the provision we need. Reflect on that truth as we close today.

DEEP DIVE

Our Daily Bread

Matthew 6:9-13 is the template Jesus gave his disciples for prayer. It is best known as the Lord's Prayer (you may have it memorized). Today we will focus on verse 11.

MISSION DEBRIEF

1.   Write down Matthew 6:11. _____

_____

_____

_____

_____

2.   Who is the giver of our daily food? _____

_____

_____

_____

_____

We thank God for our food, and we ask him to bless it before our meals. But we seldom reflect that what we eat was created by him. In a way, every time we eat, we taste the divine. Joe Rigney explains it this way: "The creation of food, tongues, and the human digestive system is the product of infinite wisdom knitting the world together in a harmonious whole, the variety of tastes creates categories and gives us edible images of divine things."[20]

"Edible images of divine things." I love that picture. How can you turn your mealtime into remembrance of God's provision in your life? How do you foresee this changing you?

---

20 Joe Rigney *The Things of Earth* p.81

DAY 5

You're My Home

Read Nehemiah 10

WE BRIEFLY IDENTIFIED ON DAY 1, WEEK 1 THE CONCEPT OF covenant. It may sound like an arcane concept, but it is something we are all fairly familiar with. For example, if you are married, you have a unique relationship with your spouse. The vows you spoke in front of friends and family might have been, "I take _____ as my husband to have and to hold from this day forward, for better, for worse, for richer, for poorer, in sickness and health, to love and to cherish, until we are parted by death. This is my solemn vow." This is a covenant relationship. You made a promise, and you were promised something as well. Marriage illustrates this picture of covenant.

Our covenant with God is slightly different. He holds to his end of the bargain regardless of what we do. Jesus is the one who helps us persevere with our end and ultimately takes responsibility for us when we fail.

As we read through Nehemiah chapter nine, we observed how the people spent a great deal of time recognizing, remembering, and repenting of the sins of their fathers. They realized that God had held up his part of the deal (covenant) and they did not. If this were a marriage, one person cheated while the other stayed faithful.

1. Read Nehemiah 9:38. What is happening? _____

_____

_____

_____

_____

MISSION DEBRIEF

2.	Why do you think it was necessary? _____

_____

_____

_____

_____

My husband and I renewed our wedding vows a couple times. It is a wonderful way to remind ourselves of the promises we made when we got married. Marriage may seem simple at first, but life and all its challenges quickly dampen the fairy tale story. The promise I made – *to have and to hold* – was not limited to sunny days but for dark days as well – *for better or for worse.*

This concept of covenantal relationship with God was not just for the Jews. When we became followers of Christ, we entered into that type of relationship.

3.	According to Mark 1:16-20, what is my promise to Jesus? _____

_____

_____

_____

_____

Do you follow him? Do you observe his teachings and apply them to your life? I struggle with that too. It is not easy, and I can get distracted and follow someone or something else. The good news is Jesus never wavers from his side of the deal.

4.	What promise is found in 2 Timothy 2:13? _____

_____

_____

_____

_____

MISSION DEBRIEF

Maybe you strayed from the path. I have, at times. Just like the Israelites, and despite the blessings God poured in my life, I decided to do things my way. The beauty of this covenant we have with God is that it cannot be broken. God is always patiently waiting for us to return.

Back to Nehemiah.

5. What is listed in Nehemiah 10:1-27? Why do you think they are there? _____

_____

_____

_____

_____

Yes, I know – another list of names. I am a strong advocate for accountability. I believe Nehemiah is writing their names down so he can remind them of their promise and make them realize the significance of this agreement.

6. Do you think accountability is necessary? Why or why not? _____

_____

_____

_____

_____

7. Glance through Nehemiah 10:28-37. What obligations of the covenant do you spot? _____

_____

_____

_____

_____

Tithes, obedience, firstfruits (check this week's H2O), separation from the rest of the world – those are a few of the obligations the Israelites agreed to. Those promises reveal their newfound commitment to be faithful to God's teachings.

MISSION DEBRIEF

8.   What is the last sentence in Nehemiah chapter 10? _____

_____

_____

_____

_____

9.   What does it mean to "not neglect the house of the Lord" (i.e., the church)? _____

_____

_____

_____

_____

Let's remember what God has done for us and remember the promise we made. When we pause and remember, we rise up as better and stronger leaders.

We have finished another week. It would seem that everything is finally coming together for Nehemiah. His backbreaking work seems to be paying off. But next week we will uncover some new drama in his life. In the meantime, pat yourself on the back for all your hard work this week.

DEEP DIVE

Psalm 16

Think of some words that describe God. Are there special words that help you describe him? A relationship is measured by what you think of the other person. The same is true for our relationship with God. Consider this uplifting and encouraging exercise: put together a well-thought-out personal statement about who God is, what he has done in our lives, and how we feel about being a Christian.

MISSION DEBRIEF

1. Finish this sentence from your own experience: God is…. _____

    _____

    _____

    _____

    _____

    David beautifully expresses his thoughts about God and what God represents to him. Look at Psalm 16, for instance.

2. Read the entire Psalm and record the attributes of God mentioned by David. _____

    _____

    _____

    _____

    _____

3. Do any of them ring solid to you as well? Which ones? _____

    _____

    _____

    _____

    _____

4. Write down verse 11. _____

    _____

    _____

    _____

    _____

MISSION DEBRIEF

5.   What does this verse mean to you today? _____

_____

_____

_____

_____

As we are nearing the end of our study, I pray you have come closer to God, and that in his presence you experience fullness of joy.

Ezra, Nehemiah, and Esther

Malachi: Champion of Faith

By Kelli Baker

Haggai was sent to the Israelites to encourage them to finish rebuilding the temple in Jerusalem. Then Ezra went into the land and taught the people the Law of the Lord. Now, around the same time as Nehemiah's governorship, God directed Malachi to rebuke the Israelites for their sinful behaviors and remind them of the wrong paths they had chosen.

Malachi did not skip a beat when he described in great detail the indiscretions of the people. The temple and the wall were rebuilt, and the covenant signed by the Levites and priests; yet the people started living in sin again. Rather than giving God their healthy animals for sacrifice, they offered blind, lame, and diseased animals as offerings to the Lord.

"Oh that there were one among you who would shut the doors, that you might not kindle fire on my altar in vain! I have no pleasure in you, says the Lord of hosts, and I will not accept an offering from your hand" (Malachi 1:10).

The Lord was angry with their behavior. As we learned this week, they had just signed a covenant to turn from their wicked ways and now they were falling back into old habits. Can you relate? How often do you find yourself making a promise to the Lord to change your behavior, but never truly repented of it? It is like saying you are sorry after you mess up, but not addressing the root of the problem.

The Israelites' half-hearted attempts at serving the Lord displeased God.

How often do we find ourselves giving the Lord only pieces of ourselves and withholding the rest?

"And you shall love the Lord your God with all your heart and with all you soul and with all your mind and with all your strength" (Mark 12:30).

MISSION DEBRIEF

God wants all of you - the good, the bad, and even the ugly.

Malachi exposed the priests' sinful behaviors as well. As leaders in the community, it was their responsibility to ensure the people were being held accountable to the Law. Rather than shepherding by wise and godly example, they were leading the people to stumble and showing partiality in matters of the Law. As women of faith, it is imperative that we are also careful not to tempt others to stumble in their faith through our own actions.

God brought to Malachi's attention the weeping and groaning of the people.

"You cover the Lord's altar with tears, with weeping and groaning, because he no longer regards the offering or accepts it with favor from your hand" (Malachi 2:13).

God would not bless their lukewarm offerings. Malachi was not admonishing simply to be confrontational and condemning. His purpose for reminding them was to encourage them to repent, admit their guilt, and turn away from their sins.

Ultimately Malachi's message points to Jesus.

"Behold, I send my messenger, and he will prepare the way before me. And the Lord whom you seek will suddenly come to his temple; and the messenger of the covenant in whom you delight, behold, he is coming, says the Lord of hosts" (Malachi 3:1).

The messenger Malachi referred to is John the Baptist. He was the first to reveal the Son of God to Israel in John 1:29-31.

God sent Malachi to prophesy of the coming of Jesus, and he was the last recorded prophet for over 400 years. Then Jesus came. God told the people through Malachi that a day was coming when evildoers would be put to shame and their roots ripped from beneath them. The reminder to "fear my name, the sun of righteousness shall rise with healing in its wings." (Malachi 4:2) was for them and their descendants to stand firm in their faith. Only then could they rise up with Jesus.

What about us? Will we stand firm in our faith until Jesus comes again?

Offering God Our Firstfruits

Habits to Outcome

By Melissa Hicks

In Nehemiah 10, we saw the Israelites rededicated themselves to offering up their firstfruits to God and refusing to neglect the temple (Nehemiah 10:35, 39b).

What are firstfruits? "The law ordered in general that the first of all ripe fruits and of liquors, or, as it is twice expressed, the first of first-fruits, should be offered in God's house (Exodus 22:29; 23:19; 34:27). It was an act of allegiance to God as the giver of all. No exact quantity was commanded, but it was left to the spiritual and moral sense of each individual."[21]

We define firstfruits as giving our first and best to God.

There are two primary areas in which we can (and should) offer God our firstfruits:

1. Money
2. Time

When we struggle to give back to God, it is often because we either don't realize that everything belongs to him (Psalm 24:1), or because we don't trust him to provide for us (Philippians 4:19). Once we have those things settled, giving is a bit easier, but it still requires intention and discipline.

There is much debate centered around tithing and the best process for giving our money to God. For more info on this topic, check out: https://www.desiringgod.org/messages/toward-the-tithe-and-beyond.

There are no hard and fast rules for a "quiet time," but we do suggest that taking a few moments in the morning to focus on God is a way you can offer him the firstfruits of your day.

---

21 Smith's Bible Dictionary, https://www.blueletterbible.org/search/dictionary/viewtopic.cfm?topic=BT0001504, accessed 8/1/20.

MISSION DEBRIEF

SUGGESTIONS FOR MORNING FIRST-FRUIT OFFERINGS:

- Greet the Lord in prayer, dedicating your day to him.

- Meditate on a verse or passage of Scripture.

- Remind yourself of gospel truths (*A Gospel Primer for Christians* by Milton Vincent is a phenomenal resource).

- Remind yourself of your identity in Christ (https://www.valmariepaper.com/embracing-biblical-view-affirmations/).

- Read a Psalm or Proverb.

- Sing (or write) a song of praise and thanksgiving to God.

Many people stop at intervals throughout the day to return focus to God. And thinking beyond just moments in the day spent with God to chunks of time such as days and weeks can feed the soul and nurture our first love.

Week 6
Rise Up for Worship

Precious Lord, take my hand
Lead me on, let me stand
I am tired, I'm weak, I am worn
Through the storm, through the night
Lead me on to the light
Take my hand, precious Lord
Lead me home[22]

Pre-1865—United States

ON A BEAUTIFUL SUNDAY AFTERNOON IN GEORGIA, A FEW
slaves gather. The regular worship service is over, and the plantation owners have already left.
They linger because they need to meet one another and share their joys, pains, and hopes. Since they
are unable to express themselves freely, religious services are, at times, the only place enslaved people
can legitimately congregate, socialize, and safely express their feelings.

Often a leader would start the session by singing a phrase, and the others would respond. Shouts
would slowly rise with the shuffling of feet and clapping of hands. Spiritual music was born. Amidst
the bondage they suffered, slaves offered God a sacrifice of praise. They were slaves on earth but found
their freedom in Jesus, and they sang about it.

You don't believe I've been redeemed,
Wade in the water
Just so the whole lake goes looking for me
God's gonna trouble the water[23]

---

22 *Take my Hand, Precious Lord* Negro Spiritual
23 *Wade in the Water* Negro Spiritual

"Spiritual songs" is derived from the King James Bible translation of Ephesians 5:19: "Speaking to yourselves in psalms and hymns and spiritual songs, singing and making melody in your heart to the Lord."[24] Worship is more than singing. Worship is what naturally flows from the heart when it is bent toward God.

Worship is not dependent on our circumstances. Our entire lives can be an act of worship.

If you are a child of God, it is time to rise up and worship.

Here We are to Worship

Have you ever finished a big project and felt a sense of accomplishment? Maybe you can finally relax since a burden is lifted off your shoulders. Yes, it is cause for rejoicing and worship.

The wall is built, Jerusalem is populated, and Nehemiah has successfully restored the people to a better place with God. It was time to rejoice and dedicate the wall. Imagine a massive party with songs, music, and people singing.

But should we only worship when life is good?

Will Things Ever Change?

Nehemiah spent twelve years in Jerusalem rebuilding. He then returned to Persia for a while, and later he asked the king for permission to check on Jerusalem. What he found was chaos and disobedience. While he had been gone, the people had slowly gone back to their old ways. When I read that chapter, I could almost hear the frustration in Nehemiah's voice.

Not one to quit, he rolled up his sleeves and started cleaning up the mess. It would have been easy for him to say, "Well, at least I tried" and head back to Persia. Instead, Nehemiah kept his eyes on God and offered his sacrifice of praise.

I heard someone once say that worship is the imitation of God. Living a life of worship will keep us from idolatry and shape us for a lifetime of obedience.

As we finish this study, let us all rise up and worship. After all, he is worthy of our praise.

---

24 https://www.loc.gov/item/ihas.200197495/#

WEEK 6

MISSION DEBRIEF

DAY 1

DAY 2

DAY 3

DAY 4

DAY 5

JOINT OP INTEL

H20

DAY 1

People Matter

Read Nehemiah 11:1 – 12:26.

LET'S KICK OFF THE WEEK WITH A TOPIC THAT IS NEAR AND DEAR to Nehemiah's heart: people. You may have guessed that today's reading is another list of names. I hope that by now you have come to appreciate the lists and their importance.

Nehemiah shows us people matter.

They mattered to Nehemiah and they matter to God.

Among the names are a selected few who uniquely gave of themselves.

1. Read Nehemiah 11:1-2. What is happening there? _____
    _____
    _____
    _____
    _____

2. What does verse 2 say happened to those men? _____
    _____
    _____
    _____

Ten percent of the population were selected to live inside the walls of Jerusalem. They went where others did not want to go. Our military today, including the Reserve and National

MISSION DEBRIEF

Guard, represent less than one percent of America's population. We, too, go where others don't go.

Nehemiah is thankful for the people who joined in the rebuilding of the nation. For Israel to be strong, Jerusalem needed to be secure. The city could only be thriving if the people inside were sound. That is why a rebuilding of their faith accompanied the rebuilding of the wall. It was now time to go to work. Notice how Nehemiah acknowledged the jobs they were doing.

3. Read the following passages and note what Nehemiah says about the persons mentioned.

    a.   Nehemiah 11:6

    b.   Nehemiah 11:12

    c.   Nehemiah 11:17

I like to get recognition for the work I do (I reckon most of us do). "Good job" is nice to hear; but I especially appreciate when someone takes the time to notice and be specific.

4. How can you show that you appreciate the people in your life? _____

_____

_____

_____

_____

Jesus took the time to notice people and recognize them.

5. Look up those passages and write down what Jesus said about them

Verses	Recognition
Mark 14:3-9	
Matthew 8:5-13	
Luke 10:38-42	

People matter. It is easy to overlook what some are doing. Let's strive to be people who notice and recognize people for the excellent jobs they are doing. A heart bent toward God will naturally love people, and our acts of love will become our "spiritual worship" (Romans 12:1). Affirming the ones who cross our path is a good start.

6.   What does Proverbs 3:27 encourage us to do? _____

_____

_____

_____

_____

7.   Whom will you recognize and honor this week? How will you do that? _____

_____

_____

_____

_____

DEEP DIVE

God Cares About You

When life gets tough, it might be tempting to conclude that God does not care about you. After all, he has better things to do, right?

That is the farthest thing from the truth. You matter to God.

1.   Read Psalm 139:1-5. How much does God know about you?_____

_____

_____

_____

_____

MISSION DEBRIEF

2. Read Psalm 56:8 and Revelation 21:4. What do they say about how much God cares for you?

_____

_____

_____

_____

It's easy to feel like we're just a face in the crowd, but that's not how God sees us. He knows us intimately. People matter to him. You matter to him.

DAY 2

Hallelujahs Here on Earth

Read Nehemiah 12:27-47.

HAVE YOU EVER PARTICIPATED IN A RIBBON-CUTTING CEREMONY? It is such a joyful experience. People gather and recognize the work accomplished and rejoice in hope for the future.

The dedication of Nehemiah's wall was a ribbon-cutting ceremony of sorts.

1. Skim through Nehemiah 12:27-47, and write down all the instances that mention singing, musical instruments, and thanksgiving. What do they say about how much God cares for you? _____

    _____

    _____

    _____

    _____

2. How would you rate the atmosphere of that day? What do they say about how much God cares for you? _____

    _____

    _____

    _____

    _____

MISSION DEBRIEF

Worship is such an essential element in our lives. It originally referred to the action of human beings in expressing homage to God because he is worthy.[25] The English word "worship" literally means worth-ship.

What reasons do those following verses give for worshipping God?

-1 Chronicles 16:25

-Isaiah 25:1

-John 9:35-38

-Philippians 2: 5-11

God is great and worthy of our worship. All our praise and devotion should be given to Jesus.

3. How do we worship God? Here are some examples (match the verse to its truth).

    John 4:23-24   worship in communion
    Acts 2:42-46   worship in truth
    I Corinthians 11:23-26   worship in fellowship with other believers

_____

_____

_____

_____

_____

25 Marshall, I. H. (1996). Worship. In D. R. W. Wood, A. R. Millard, J. I. Packer, & D. J. Wiseman (Eds.), *New Bible dictionary* (3rd ed., p. 1250). Leicester, England; Downers Grove, IL: InterVarsity Press.

MISSION DEBRIEF

4. Obedience is also an act of worship. Obeying Jesus' teachings demonstrates that we love him and trust him. How does Romans 12:1 convey that truth? _____

_____

_____

_____

_____

The Israelites dedicated the wall. It was an act of worship in which they declared that the wall was not theirs but God's.

5. Have you ever considered that dedicating something to God is an act of worship? _____

_____

_____

_____

_____

6. Is there something you can dedicate to God today? Is it your child? Your spouse? A project? Your work? _____

_____

_____

_____

_____

7. Rewrite Colossians 3:17 in the first person as a prayer of dedication. _____

_____

_____

_____

_____

MISSION DEBRIEF

DEEP DIVE

Idolatry

What happens when we worship something or someone other than God? We are then guilty of idolatry. Brian Rosner defines idolatry as "an attack on God's exclusive rights to our love, trust, and obedience."[26]

In today's world, the word idol is commonly used for movie stars, musicians, and athletes. An idol is anything that replaces God in your life. I encourage you to check out this week's H2O to identify and get rid of your idols.

So, why is God against idols?

1. What insight does Exodus 20:2-6 give us about idols? _____

    _____

    _____

    _____

    _____

2. What dangers are there in worshipping idols instead of God, according to Romans 1:21-25?_

    _____

    _____

    _____

    _____

We are guilty of idolatry when we put more emphasis on the creation rather than the Creator.

The root issue of idolatry is self or selfishness.

---

26 https://www.biblicalstudies.org.uk/pdf/idolatry_rosner.pdf

MISSION DEBRIEF

"I love the creation for what it can do for me and the perceived control I have over it." Take money, for example. "I love money because I can buy things that make me feel good or because it gives me a sense of security about the future." There is nothing wrong with having money, but the source of my happiness and security needs to be found in God, not money.

3.   What did Jesus say about money in Matthew 6:24? _____

_____

_____

_____

_____

Does this mean we need to sell everything, move to a monastery, and adopt John the Baptist's dress code (Matthew 3:4)? By no means. God wants us to enjoy his creation. After all, he calls it good (Genesis 1:31). The worship of God is the result of a relationship based on love. I worship him and him alone because he is the source of everything in my life. Creation is good, but God is greater.

4.   What can you do today to ensure you are worshipping the Creator and not the creation? ____

_____

_____

_____

_____

DAY 3

When Worship Turns Sour

Read Nehemiah 13:1-18.

THE 1993 COMEDY GROUNDHOG DAY[27] FEATURES A GRUMPY weatherman, played by Bill Murray, who covers the annual Groundhog Day event in Pennsylvania. Trapped in a time loop, he finds himself reliving the events of February 2nd over and over again.

I have experienced the feeling of being stuck in unhealthy patterns. Maybe you have too. Perhaps, like me, you have moved to a new place and hoped for a fresh start, only to find out that issues, controversies, and gossip have followed you. You long for change, but you get stuck dealing with the same old stuff.

After twelve years in Jerusalem, Nehemiah returned to Persia. He did not stay long, but it was enough time for the situation to deteriorate back in Jerusalem.

Some habits are hard to break.

Habits are patterns that shape every aspect of our lives. They form our routine, and more often than not, we are not even aware of them. According to a study by researchers at Tel Aviv University, "predictable, repetitive routines are calming and help reduce anxiety. They'll also help you take control of your day and, subsequently, your life."[28] But some habits are unhealthy. For example, eating ice cream every afternoon can make the bathroom scale tip in the wrong direction. Nevertheless, we must struggle to stop that habit even though it brings us comfort.

Bad habits can quickly turn into sinful behaviors if left unchecked. The Bible has a term for deeply ingrained sins: strongholds.

When Nehemiah returned to Jerusalem, he quickly saw that matters had gone back to the way they were before.

---

27 More appropriate for teens and up

28 https://www.piedmont.org/living-better/why-routines-are-good-for-your-health#:~:text=According%20to%20a%20study%20by,Start%20your%20day%20off%20right.

MISSION DEBRIEF

1. Read Nehemiah 13:4. Describe what is going on. _____

    _____

    _____

    _____

    _____

2. What is his reaction in Nehemiah 13:8-9? Is he justified in his anger? Why or why not? ____

    _____

    _____

    _____

    _____

3. What other issues is he dealing with, according to Nehemiah 13:10-11? _____

    _____

    _____

    _____

    _____

4. Read Nehemiah 10:39. What promise were they breaking? _____

    _____

    _____

    _____

    _____

MISSION DEBRIEF

5. What is the final issue that Nehemiah is addressing in verses 15-18? What reminder is he

    giving them about the dangers of disobedience? _____

    _____

    _____

    _____

    _____

We finished last week's homework with the topic of covenantal relationship. The truth of the matter is that in my relationship with God, I will always fall short. It would be easy for me to shake my head at the story in Nehemiah and pass a quick judgment. How can they so quickly forget and return to their old ways? Unfortunately, I, too, do that. Left to my own devices, I can do no good. Thankfully, I have Jesus to help me.

6. What does Romans 7:10 say about our human nature? _____

    _____

    _____

    _____

    _____

7. We may not have the ability to succeed on our own, but who does, according to

    Ephesians 1:19? _____

    _____

    _____

    _____

    _____

MISSION DEBRIEF

8. How does 2 Corinthians 10:3-6 equip us to break strongholds? _____

_____

_____

_____

_____

Nehemiah was an outstanding leader, but he did not have the power to change the hearts and minds of the people. Only God can do that. Do you have strongholds in your life? Maybe you feel that you should continue to keep things a secret, wear a mask, and hide the pain. Or perhaps you believe that if you only try harder, you can beat it on your own. God is saying the opposite.

9. What beautiful truth is stated in James 5:16? _____

_____

_____

_____

_____

10. What are you struggling with right now? Whom can you confess to and ask for prayer?_____

_____

_____

_____

_____

We break strongholds when God is at the center in our lives. Bad habits are merely an indication that we are worshiping the wrong things. Together with Christ, we can demolish the strongholds that prevent us from rising up.

MISSION DEBRIEF

DEEP DIVE

Use Dynamite.

Alfred Nobel invented dynamite in 1867. It quickly gained popularity and replaced black powder in the mining, quarrying, construction, and demolition industries.

Read Acts 1:9. The word translated "power" is the Greek word *dynamis*, from which we get our English word, dynamite.

To successfully demolish strongholds, we need to use spiritual dynamite. I suggest two forms: prayer and God's Word.

1. With what does Ephesians 6:17 compare the Word of God to? _____

   _____

   _____

   _____

   _____

2. What does Psalm 119:105 reveal? _____

   _____

   _____

   _____

   _____

3. How did Jesus resist the devil in Matthew 4:1-11? _____

   _____

   _____

   _____

   _____

4. The sword is the ONLY offensive weapon at our disposal. How can we use it? _____

_____

_____

_____

_____

Available 24/7, prayer is our instant and direct connection with God. Throughout our study, we have observed how Nehemiah repeatedly turned to God in prayer. When you combine the Word of God with prayer to fight your stronghold(s), you are using two sticks of spiritual dynamite. Turning scripture into prayer has been a game-changer for me.[29] I believe I better align with God's will when I pray his words back to him.

Here are a few suggestions for praying God's Word:

Stronghold	Verses
Idolatry	1 Chronicles 29:11; Psalm 145:16; 1 Corinthians 8:6
Addiction	Psalm 139:23-24; 1 John 1:9
Depression	Psalm 42:5-6; Lamentations 3:21-23; Romans 5:5

Give it a try. It might change your life too.

---

29 I recommend *Praying God's Word* by Beth Moore. It is a great resource on that topic.

What is Done in Secret

Read Nehemiah 13:19-30.

THE MERRIAM WEBSTER DICTIONARY DEFINES INTEGRITY AS "firm adherence to a code of especially moral or artistic values: incorruptibility." You may have people in your life who display this quality. You might have been described as a person of integrity. Uprightness is evident in our lives when we practice it all the time. We covered the concept of hypocrisy in week three, day three. Who I am in public needs to match who I am in private. What you do when no one is watching says a lot more about you than any virtuous deeds performed in public.

ABOUT MIXED MARRIAGES

What Nehemiah is referring to in Nehemiah 13:19, and Nehemiah 10:30 is a command God gave Moses in Deuteronomy 7:1-5. It is **NOT** saying that we cannot marry someone from a different race. It is telling us that we should not be unequally yoked.

That same concept is explained in 2 Corinthians 6:14. It is not wise to marry an unbeliever.

From the beginning of this study, it has been evident that Nehemiah was a man of integrity.

1. What do you think was the source of Nehemiah's integrity? Why did he choose to live a righteous life? _____

_____

_____

_____

_____

MISSION DEBRIEF

The people of Jerusalem lacked integrity. As soon as no one was watching, they acted selfishly. Nehemiah put on his drill sergeant hat and tried to talk some sense into them.

2. Read Nehemiah 13:19-22. How is Nehemiah trying to protect them? _____

_____

_____

_____

_____

3. In Nehemiah 13:25-26, he confronts them regarding mixed marriages. How is he trying to

change the situation? _____

_____

_____

_____

_____

4. In what ways have you felt this level of frustration? _____

_____

_____

_____

5. Can you force people to do the right thing? What can you do?_____

_____

_____

_____

_____

MISSION DEBRIEF

Integrity does not come by osmosis. It is a resolve to do the right thing no matter the consequence and no matter the audience.

6.   How did these biblical characters display integrity?

Genesis 15:6	
1 Samuel 1:11/1 Samuel 1:24-28	
Esther 4:13-17	
Daniel 1:8-9	
Acts 7:59-60	

How do we become women of integrity? First, we need to recognize the source of integrity.

7.   Why should we display integrity according to 1 Peter 1:16? _____

_____

_____

_____

_____

8.   What does Psalm 25:8 say about the source of our integrity? _____

_____

_____

_____

_____

9.   What instructions can be found in Psalm 119:9-11?_____

_____

_____

_____

_____

MISSION DEBRIEF

Character is not grown overnight. It is a lifelong pursuit, but there is a bonus for doing the right thing when no one is watching.

10.   Read the following verses and list the benefit(s).

  • Matthew 6:3-4
  • Matthew 6:6
  • Matthew 6:17-18

_____

_____

_____

_____

_____

God knows, and God sees. When my heart is bent towards him, and I have an attitude of worship, I will display integrity. Nehemiah's sole purpose was to obey God and serve his people.

11.   Write down the very last sentence of Nehemiah. _____

_____

_____

_____

_____

12.   Can this be your attitude? Would you be content to be solely remembered by God? _____

_____

_____

_____

_____

MISSION DEBRIEF

DEEP DIVE

How Do I Get Closer to God?

The most difficult journeys are not necessarily the longest. Mine is 18 inches long: the distance between my head and my heart. How do I bridge the gap between distance and intimacy? How can my faith be experiential and not solely intellectual?

1. How about you? Have you ever struggled with that?_____

   _____

   _____

   _____

   _____

Connecting with an invisible God is not easy. We all know that God is here and everywhere, but how do I make that fact a reality that stirs my heart and fuels my prayers? How do I share my fears and hope with the Master of the universe?

Let's ask Hannah (you can read her story in 1 Samuel). She is childless. Her husband does not understand her and thinks his love should be enough. His other wife taunts her because she cannot have children. And when she goes to the temple to pour out her soul, the priest thinks she's drunk!

2. Has there been a time when you were misunderstood and lonely? Briefly describe._____

   _____

   _____

   _____

   _____

God knows, understands, and is ever-present. He hears Hannah, and she gives birth to a child – Samuel. True to her promise, she surrendered her child to God.

MISSION DEBRIEF

3. Write down 1 Samuel 2:2. _____
    _____
    _____
    _____
    _____

    Notice how Hannah switches from the third person to the second person in her prayer.

4. Fill in the blanks:

    There is none holy like _____ For there is none besides _____

    In just two short sentences, Hannah bridges the gap between distance and intimacy. There is none other than God. He does not exist because I believe in him.

    He is, because he is God.

    I exist because he does.

    Nothing exists outside of him.

    What does Romans 1:20 say about how God reveals himself to us?

    God is, and there is none like him. Can you make that your daily faith builder? And "God will drive our faith, like a stake, from our head to our heart. And we will never be the same again."[30]

---

30 https://www.desiringgod.org/articles/the-distance-between-head-and-heart

DAY 5

Have My Heart

SWEET FRIEND, WE HAVE REACHED THE END OF OUR STUDY. What a journey! Nehemiah has taken us many places and forced us to look deep in our souls to awaken the leader within us. Before we conclude, I want to take you on one last pit stop. But first, let's reflect on a few points.

I hope you have come to appreciate Nehemiah and the example he set for us.

1. How would you describe his leadership style? _____

    _____

    _____

    _____

    _____

2. What lessons has he taught you? _____

    _____

    _____

    _____

MISSION DEBRIEF

3. What is your biggest takeaway? _____

_____

_____

_____

_____

We have learned about his devotion to God, his successes, his frustrations, and his failures. He gave us excellent pointers on leadership, but he is not the one we should follow. The final place I want to take you is the cross.

Jesus is the one we follow. He is the one who gives us our mission orders.

4. Our orders can be found in Matthew 28:18-20. What are we to do? _____

_____

_____

_____

_____

5. What is our motivation for following the orders according to John 14:15? How is this an act of worship?_____

_____

_____

_____

_____

MISSION DEBRIEF

6.   Read John 14:16-18. Are we alone on this mission? _____

_____

_____

_____

_____

7.   Let's be specific for a minute. What do you sense God asking you to do right now? How does

that make you feel? What is one step you can take this week to rise up to the call? _____

_____

_____

_____

_____

We obey because we love him. We love because he first loved us. We worship him because he is the source of everything. He was there in the beginning, and through him everything was created (John 1:1-3). He equips us with the proper tools to face opposition and fight for justice. He revives our hearts and calls us to remember his provision. A lifetime of obedience starts with surrender. *Not my will, but yours be done.*

And we are never alone.

8.   That beautiful promise can be found in Deuteronomy 31:6. Write it down in your own

words. _____

_____

_____

_____

_____

MISSION DEBRIEF

9.   Will you rise up and answer the call? Take the lessons learned in Nehemiah and apply them to your life. Remember: There is a place for you at the wall. _____

_____

_____

_____

_____

DEEP DIVE

Build on the Rock

To rise properly, we need a strong foundation. Any building with a shaky foundation will not stand for long. Thankfully, we have in Jesus the surest and strongest foundation.

1.   Read Ephesians 2:19-22.

   a.   Who is the cornerstone? _____

   b.   What are we building on? _____

   c.   What is the purpose of this building? _____

What a beautiful promise and an incredible picture Ephesians 2:19-22 paints. It reminds me of a song I used to sing in church

Lord prepare me
To be a sanctuary
Pure and holy
Tried and true
And with thanksgiving
I'll be a living
Sanctuary for You

We need Jesus. Without him, we are sheep gone astray.

MISSION DEBRIEF

2.   Read Matthew 6:24-25.

    a.   How do we build on the rock? _____

    _____

    b.   What are the benefits? _____

    _____

Rain, wind, opposition, hardships, injustice, nothing can throw us off course. Armed with that knowledge, we can confidently rise up and worship.

Would you finish this study with one last reading? One final act of worship? Read Psalm 61 out loud. Make this your parting prayer.

So will I ever sing praises to your name,
As I perform my vows day after day.
Psalm 61:8

Jesus: Our Object of Worship

By Kelli Baker

Over the past five weeks we have studied examples of excellent leadership. However, the ultimate goal as Christ followers is to be more like Jesus. During his time on earth, he demonstrated what it means to seek God's will and live a God-fearing life. Fully man and fully God, Jesus dealt with the same struggles we deal with today. He rose up to the call and set the example for us.

The Call

Jesus' calling was to come to earth and save God's people from their sins. He lived a life fully devoted to his ministry, and he knew his ultimate fate. Shortly before he sacrificed his life for us, Jesus cried out, "Abba, Father, all things are possible for you. Remove this cup from me. Yet not what I will, but what you will." (Mark 14:36). He knew that in order to fulfill God's purpose for his life, he would have to die in the most excruciating way. Yet he still surrendered everything to God's will.

Opposition

Not immune to opposition either, Jesus showed us how to rise up when faced with disapproval. When Jesus went to fast and pray alone in the wilderness, the enemy began attacking him. Jesus responded by quoting scripture. Each time the enemy tried to tempt Jesus, he would reply with, "It is written." As Christ followers, it is imperative that we arm ourselves with the wisdom and knowledge of God's Word, so we can fight against opposition.

Justice

The Pharisees were constantly trying to trap Jesus. When they brought Jesus a woman who had committed adultery, Jesus responded as Nehemiah would have. Rather than reacting to their demand to bring charges against the woman, he paused. "Jesus bent down and wrote with his finger on the ground" (John 8:6b). The Pharisees persisted.

Jesus' response exemplified wisdom and justice. "Let him who is without sin among you be the first to throw a stone at her" (John 8:7b). Jesus stood up for the humiliated woman, instead of being pulled into their trap.

Revival

Jesus' Sermon on the Mount was his revival in the land – much like Ezra's example in Nehemiah 8. He reiterated the laws they had previously been taught, and he finished by saying, "Do not think that I have come to abolish the Law or the Prophets; I have not come to abolish them but to fulfill them." (Matthew

Remember

Jesus told his disciples that whoever loves him will keep his commandments. He also promised his disciples that he would send the Holy Spirit to be their helper so they could remember all that had been taught to them.

"But the Helper, the Holy Spirit, whom the Father will send in my name, he will teach you all things and bring to your remembrance all that I have said to you" (John

We too are recipients of those promises. He sent his Spirit to live in us as well, so we would have an advocate reminding us of God's truths. Only through the Spirit of God can we align our lives with his will.

Worship

Finally, we are called to rise up and worship. The Gospels provide several examples of how Jesus calls us to worship him. Let's look at Martha and Mary for example. When Jesus visited them, Mary sat at his feet. While she rested and listened to Jesus, Martha was distracted with the details of serving. She complained about Mary's lack of help, but Jesus reminded her of the better choice,

"Martha, Martha, you are anxious and troubled about many things, but one thing is necessary. Mary has chosen the good portion, which will not be taken away from her" (Luke 10:41-42).

Jesus told Martha that Mary was the one who was worshiping as she should. Worship doesn't necessarily mean constantly singing songs of praise. It can be a grateful word to God while cleaning the house or driving down the road. It can mean adoring God for the beautiful sunrise he so masterfully creates each morning. It may be a silent moment before you begin your day. Finding ways throughout your day to reflect on God's goodness and showing him your gratitude is true worship.

Jesus came to this earth to provide us an eternity with him. We do not deserve this great gift, yet he graciously gives it. He is worthy of all our praise and worship.

Identifying Idols

Habits to Outcome

By Melissa Hicks

When Nehemiah came back to Jerusalem after being away for many years, he saw how the Jewish people had strayed from the Lord. It's easier for us to wander away from God than we might realize.

"An idol is anything or anyone that begins to capture our hearts, minds, and affections more than God."[31]

You might not think you have any idols in your life, but here are a few questions to assess your risk.

- Am I willing to sin to get this?
- Am I willing to sin if I think I'm going to lose this?
- Do I turn to this as a refuge and comfort instead of going to God?

"When we cease to worship God, we do not worship nothing. We worship anything."[32]

QUESTIONS TO ASK SOMEONE ELSE ABOUT YOURSELF:

- What do you see me running to instead of God?
- Where do you see a demanding spirit in me?
- What do you see me clinging to and craving more than God?
- Where do you see me wanting something so badly that I'm willing to sin to get it or to keep it?

It's not enough to identify idols. You have to get rid of them.

---

31 Bigney, Brad. *Gospel Treason: Betraying the Gospel with Hidden Idols* (Phillipsburg, New Jersey: P&R Publishing, 2012), 24.
32 Bigney, Brad. *Gospel Treason: Betraying the Gospel with Hidden Idols* (Phillipsburg, New Jersey: P&R Publishing, 2012), 33.

H$_2$O

STEPS TO DESTROY IDOLS:

- List the idols you've identified.

- Pray and fast, asking God to show you how to think and act differently in these areas.

- Make a specific plan to starve your idol (include the little choices you might not think matter).

- Ask God for strength to feed your worship of him, rather than your idols.

- Soak in Scripture.

CONCLUSION

A little railroad engine was employed about a station yard for such work as it was built for, pulling a few cars on and off the switches. One morning it was waiting for the next call when a long train of freight cars asked a large engine in the roundhouse to take it over the hill. "I can't; that is too much a pull for me," said the great engine built for hard work. Then the train asked another engine, and another, only to hear excuses and be refused. In desperation, the train asked the little switch engine to draw it up the grade and down the other side. "I think I can," puffed the little locomotive, and put itself in front of the great heavy train. As it went on, the little engine kept bravely puffing faster and faster, "I think I can, I think I can, I think I can."

As it neared the top of the grade, which had so discouraged the larger engines, it went more slowly. However, it still kept saying, "I—think—I—can, I—think—I—can." It reached the top by drawing on bravery and then went on down the grade, congratulating itself by saying, "I thought I could, I thought I could."[33]

THIS 1930 FAIRYTALE HAS BEEN A FAVORITE TO MANY GENERATIONS of children – and adults too. When the mountain in front of you is bigger than anything you ever faced, do you say to yourself, "I think I can"? Nehemiah did. He might have been the smaller engine, but he did not wait for the bigger ones to make things happen.

It feels like only yesterday that we started on this journey through Nehemiah. It is my hope and prayer that you have been encouraged, challenged, moved, and changed. I know that time spent studying the Word is never wasted. It always bears fruit. I know that because God says so.

---

33 *The Little Engine That Could* by Watty Piper, 1930

For as the rain and the snow come down from heaven
and do not return there but water the earth,
making it bring forth and sprout,
giving seed to the sower and bread to the eater,
so shall my word be that goes out from my mouth;
it shall not return to me empty,
but it shall accomplish that which I purpose,
and shall succeed in the thing for which I sent it.

Isaiah 55:10-11

I wish we could sit down together over a cup of coffee (or tea or water. I'm not picky!). I would love to hear what God has taught you and what he has shown you over those past six weeks. We can learn so much from each other. Isn't that the beauty of the Church, how we all need one another? Nehemiah built a wall, but he could not have done it alone. He needed priests, masons, jewelers, carpenters, men, and women. Everyone was mission-essential.

A few days before he was crucified, Jesus told his hardheaded disciples that he would destroy the temple and rebuild it in three days. Crazy, right?! But he did. And he became the cornerstone, our foundation to build on. He is still building his Church today, and he needs everybody to join-- enlisted, officers, retired, active duty, Reserve, Guard, wives, mom, children. We all have a place at his wall.

The journey has steep climbs and scary curves, but it also has mountaintop views and fellow sojourners.

It will not always be easy, but *I think I can* because greater is he who is within us than he who is in the world (1 John 4.4).

How about you? Do you think you can?

—MURIEL GREGORY
Fort Leavenworth
Leavenworth, Kansas